SUPER EASY AND QUICK
AIR FRYER

COOKBOOK FOR BEGINNERS

Lots of healthy and mouthwatering recipes, each illustrated by vivid full-colour images, simple to prepare using UK ingredients and measurements

Clara Foxley

TABLE OF CONTENTS

INTRODUCTION

In the year 2010, a man Fred van der Weij invented the air fryer. Van der Weij was a Dutch inventor and an entrepreneur. He got the idea from the worldwide famous snack – French fries. He aimed at developing a more nutritious and enjoyable version of this sweet without losing their flavour or consistency. Therefore, it brought about the invention of the air fryer. This clever gadget cooks food using super-heated air and rapid air circulation to achieve crispy exterior and tender interior without any oil.

Air-frying was initially introduced as an alternative way of making healthy French fries and today it has grown into an all-inclusive cooking equipment. This is why we have this cookbook. The Super Easy and Quick Air Fryer Cookbook for Beginners is meant to accompany you on your adventure of trying out different kinds of foods such as appetizers, main course, side dishes, and dessert options.
This is a cook book with easy but delicious recipes fit for beginners which caters for different tastes and diets. Expect classic cravings in addition to unique concoctions for your appetite surprises.

We know that exploring new appliances is a daunting task that requires lots of work. This is why we develop recipes that have brief duration of preparation and cooking. The recipes feature step-by-step directions and easy-to-find ingredients so that you can make tasty dishes which even fussiest of members of the family may appreciate.

So go ahead! Engage the fantastic advantages entailed by air frying such as less fatty foods or meal portions taken, quicker clean-up activity following the cooking procedure, and minimal time consumption. This should be the key that will open up unlimited culinary possibilities to your oven, turning every dish into a specialty.

WHY THE AIR FRYER?

Today, UK households have embraced the air fryer as one of the most useful gadgets available in their kitchens. The air fryer provides a quick, healthy alternative for making a multitude of tasty yet healthy diet foods using little fat. This chapter will discuss advantages of using an air fryer, compare it with the conventional frying method, and how this new appliance does work.

BENEFITS OF USING AN AIR FRYER

An air fryer has numerous benefits that justify adding it in the kitchen. Here are some of the key benefits:

1. HEALTHIER MEALS: The air fryer is a product that allows creation of minimally oiled versions of deep roasted favourite foods. The air fryer will help you prepare your food crispy but with as low as 80% of fat than when deep frying will submerge your food in oil.

2. FASTER COOKING TIMES: Combination of the compactness of the air fryers and high-speed fan that circulates the hot air evenly around the food, enables this machine to cook foods faster compared with the conventional oven methods.

3. LESS LINGERING ODOURS: An air fryer which works under a closed system with efficient filters emits fewer lingering smells than frying in a cooking pan on a stove top.

4. EASY CLEAN-UP: The cleaning of the machine happens to be the simplest following your culinary venture due to the non-stick basket or tray design of the machine. Most of them include dish washable components for maximum convenience.

5. SPACE SAVER: Most air fryers have a compact designing, which makes them easy and suitable for small kitchen counter spaces as well.

COMPARISON WITH TRADITIONAL FRYING

Now let's compare air frying with traditional methods in terms of health benefits, efficiency, and taste:

1. HEALTH: It has already been noted that one of the biggest benefits of air frying is a decrease in fat in the final product. This means lower calories, minimal guilt, and indulgence in formerly deep-fried snacks. This also leads to less oil that in turn reduces saturated fats that are good for the heart.
2. EFFICIENCY: Furthermore, such fryers are usually more energy efficient since they typically fry food faster than oven frying or stove top frying. This speed advantage is extremely critical for busy homes or people with less time.
3. TASTE: Even though some may argue that the flavour of air-fried foods is nothing like real fried food and may disappoint users, most users confirm that the product obtained resembles the authentic crispiness. Air frying also gives flexibility in terms of adjusting factors like temperature and time in order to attain desired results.

BASICS ON HOW AN AIR FRYER WORKS

To appreciate why air fryers continue to win hearts and tastebuds, it's essential to understand how they function:
Air fryer is a small-sized countertop gadget which is used for cooking food through circulation of hot atmosphere about it giving rise to an outer covering like that of deep-fried food yet without drowning it in oil. This is done by putting heat element and cooling through circulating of hot air at high speed.

This food cooking process is actually based on the so called Maillard reaction, which leads to developing both crusty crust and pleasant aroma of the fries. This takes place as the heated air hits its temperature at 140 to 165 degrees Celsius on the top or exterior surface of the food inside the air fryer basket/tray, which forms a very appealing golden-brown colour on the outside.

An air fryer usually comes with a variable thermostat and timer for easy adjustment of cooking according to the particular food being cooked. They are also conveniently sized and heat up fast which is good news for those meals that you love.

CHOOSING THE RIGHTW

The United Kingdom market has numerous brands and varieties; hence, it may prove difficult in identifying the perfect choice that will be ideal for your needs. We will look at different points of choosing an air fryer, famous brands and models and also will take into account recommendations for maintenance and cleansing in this chapter.

FACTORS TO CONSIDER WHEN PURCHASING AN AIR FRYER

1. **CAPACITY:** The size of an air fryer also determines the number of food items that it can fit in. Think about how many persons are you going to feed–some families will require larger capacities (4 litres or more) whereas little families may need a mini oven (2-3 litres).

2. **POWER:** The power level of an air fryer influences how fast it cooks food and how efficient the fryer is in doing so. The majority of units sold in the UK are between 800 and 2000 watts. High power rated devices will tend to heat quickly and uniformly while utilizing a lot of energy.

3. **TEMPERATURE CONTROL:** Quality air frying also allows for the setting of specific temperature that ranges between 180 and 200 degrees Celsius. Exact temperature control will enable your meal to be cooked in the centre whereas its outer parts will remain crispy.

4. **TIMER:** For that reason, a timer is necessary as it comes with an option of auto-shut off that helps in mitigating cases of oversized or burnt food. Choose models that have timers of thirty to sixty minutes at a minimum.

5. **EXTRA FEATURES:** Air fryers also have other options such as grilling, baking or roasting which are used to prepare different types of food.

POPULAR BRANDS AND MODELS IN THE UK MARKET

1. **PHILIPS:** One renowned brand that makes top notch air fryers is Phillips with Philips Air fryer XXL HD9650 having starfish-shaped twin-turbo cyclonic design for fast and efficient circulation of air. For a family it is quite capacious – 1.4 kilograms.

2. **TEFAL:** Another leading UK consumer favourite is in this ActiFry range. The Tefal Tefal ActiFry Genius XL comes with an innovative paddle design that guarantees equal cooking, and a little oil. It is user friendly due to its 9 automatic cooking programme and simple controls.

3. **NINJA:** These air fryers are very popular because of their ability to cook food using little oil. They have lots of features including a model called the Ninja Foodi 9-in-1 multi-Cooker with a 5.7 litres capacity, nine cooking modes and accurate temperatures.

4. **COSORI:** Cosori is a household name in air fryers. It offers cheap but effective units such as the Cosori Air Fryer CP137-AF having eleven pre-set cooking mode options, dishwasher safe components and compact design ideal for small spaces.

MAINTENANCE AND CLEANING TIPS

One should always undertake routine cleaning of this machine in order for it to perform optimally and serve for a long time. Follow these tips to keep your air fryer in top condition:

1. **UNPLUG THE APPLIANCE BEFORE CLEANING:** Safety first, before carrying out cleanliness is to disconnect an air fryer for you.

2. **CLEAN THE FRYING BASKET AND PAN AFTER EVERY USE:** Soak the frying basket and pan in warm water mixed with soap, use a mild soft sponge to scrub every last bit of food particle residues or traces of oil.

3. **WIPE DOWN THE INTERIOR:** Put water on a wet cloth and clean inside the air fryer without leaving any food bits.

4. **CLEAN THE HEATING ELEMENT IF REQUIRED:** If you use an air fryer and discover stuck food, clean it out with a gentle brush. Hence, be very careful and avoid breaking any of the component.

5. **REGULARLY INSPECT THE APPLIANCE:** Regularly test every broken part and non-working feature of your Air Fryer and replace it quickly.

PREHEATING, TEMPERATURE CONTROLS, AND COOKING TIMES

In the decision-making process for an Air Fryer, some important considerations include; preheating and temperature options. Therefore, a perfect Air Fryer must be equipped with the fast pre-heat function and this is because, it lowers almost all of your required cooking time especially on comparison with other oven types. Ensure that you get a model with three-minute quick preheat which allows for retention of the fresh taste of your food items.

Many air fryers are also equipped with a temperature adjuster for different recipes and settings. One should consider getting an appliance with wide operating temperature which ranges from low to high setting. That way, you can fry anything like chicken wings or even handle very delicate pastries.

Air Fryer cooking times differ according to the device's model, as well as the intricacy of your meal. However, getting a model which has an inbuilt timer saves you from overcooking and undercooking of your food. Select a timer depending on your preference that ranges between thirty as well as sixty minutes.

SAFETY PRECAUTIONS

The primary consideration should be your safety when dealing with any kitchen equipment. Safety is also very essential in that you should check for auto shut-off features and cool-to-touch exterior among others when choosing the ideal Air Fryer.

1.   AUTO SHUT-OFF: You are protected from such an eventuality by automatic shutdown of the device at the stipulated moment that guards against burnt food and kitchen fire.

2.   COOL-TO-TOUCH EXTERIORS: The Air Fryers discharge a huge level of warmth during operation and avoiding heat insulated models could result in scalding and accidents. Ensure that the handle, outside, and all controls stay cool throughout the baking.

COMMON AIR FRYER MISTAKES AND HOW TO AVOID THEM

The functions of the Air Fryer can also be affected by some common mistakes that people do. Learning how to avoid those mistakes will result in better cooked meals and longer lasting Air Fryers.

1.   OVERCROWDING THE BASKET: Stuffing lots of food items in to the air fryer basket is another huge mistake we should avoid. They limit even cooking making it possible to get only partly cooked dishes. Leave some room in between your food items to allow for adequate air circulation.

2.   NOT SHAKING OR TURNING THE FOOD: Fries and tiny snacks, too, need to be turned over once to achieve equal crispiness. Gently turning them helps to achieve an even fry and crust for the products that are relatively larger like chicken of fish fillets.

3.   IGNORING MAINTENANCE: It is important to clean your air fryer after every use. Thus, it prevents burnt food particles from remaining on the surface of your appliances to preserve their quality for future cooking sessions.

4.   USING EXCESSIVE OIL: Air frying is one of the key advantages of these appliances because it helps prepare meals that are lower in fat compared to deep-fried foods. Nonetheless, using too much oil negates the advantage and makes it hard to get the desired outcome. Ensure that you stick to recommended quantities or use sprays.

5.   COOKING MULTIPLE TYPES OF FOOD TOGETHER: Multitasking appears convenient, but cooking various foods that need different periods of time do not give balanced results. Ensure you cook similar items together or a simple rule "cook what takes time first then add the shorter/quicker cooking item".

UNDERSTANDING INGREDIENTS
for the Air Fryer

FOODS THAT ARE BEST SUITED FOR AIR FRYING

The Air Fryer, with its speedy circulation of superheated air around food gives a crisp outside without lots of oil. Many staple foods cooked in UK households fare well in this unique cooking environment:

1. FROZEN FOODS: In many supermarkets, the pre-fried and frozen food items like chips, onion rings or chicken nuggets are cooked just perfect without even a need to defrost them. They may also add a little tiny of oil so as to make them crunchier.

2. VEGETABLES: Air Fryers make roasting vegetables like sweet potatoes, cherry tomatoes, bell peppers, or Brussel sprouts very easy; just toss some oil and spices and they are ready to eat.

3. MEAT: These juices cut like bacon or lamb chops which give just the right amount of drips for natural crunch when air-fried.

4. SEAFOOD: The same is true when cooking other daintier alternatives like salmon fillet or breaded fish. These ingredients are usually easily cooked evenly and at high speed for a short time to ensure that they retain moisture in their centre part but develop a flavourful crust.

WHAT TO AVOID: FOODS THAT DON'T FRY WELL

Using an air fryer may require some trial and error as not all dishes cook equally well in it:

1. WET BATTER: Air Fryers don't produce optimum results for foods which have a wet, gluey type of batter such as traditional British fish and chips or tempura.

2. LEAFY GREENS: Air-fried delicate and thin vegetables like spinach or kale easily get dried up or burned down.

3. CHEESE: Direct melting of cheese on the cooker's mesh basket may lead to chaos since the melted cheese tends to stick, run, and ooze through. One thing to note here is that if you want to combine cheese with your meals, then melt it over already cooked foods.

4. LARGE CUTS OF MEAT: The Air Fryer may provide uneven or under-cooked larger pieces of meat which are best cooked in a slow cooker.

HOW TO ADAPT TRADITIONAL RECIPES FOR THE AIR FRYER

For those who have a love affair with British meals, modifying conventional recipes for the Air Fryer is a cakewalk. Here are some simple steps you can follow to transform your favourite dishes into Air Fryer masterpieces:

1. First, you should choose appropriate cuisines that you wish to imitate in your Air Fryer. Check for oven baked and deep-fried food because that's what the air fryer does-cook with hot air circulation.

2. Some traditional recipes may contain big portions or strange shapes, which do not fit into the Air Fryer's small size and therefore cannot be cooked in an air fryer. Cut food in pieces of approximately equal size so that you can cook each piece of your meal at a similar rate.

3. Since air fryer is much faster than oven or stove for cooking purpose so you should adjust your cooking time according to it. Overall, lower the cooking temperature by 15 degrees Celsius and cut cooking time by about 20% comparing with common practice – but always watch over the food until it has reached the desired level of doneness.

4. Inadequate filling of the basket can interfere with air flow resulting in non-uniform final result. Alternatively, try cooking in small quantities or buy another basket for large meals instead.

5. Air Fryers require a less coating of o compared to deep-fried recipes which are generally saturated with oil. Try other cooking sprays or give breadcrumb-coating instead of traditional batter that gives you crisper texture.

6. Some conventional dishes require special utensils which may not be inserted straight into the Air Fryer directly. Ensure you purchase a specially-designed accessory kit that can feature unique pans, trays, or other internal parts.

7. You should see to it that the recipe you adopt for this case must not be an ordinary recipe that can just cook traditionally without a touch of science! However, don't hesitate to adjust timings, temperatures, and techniques until you find what works best for your situation.

THE HEALTHY EDGE:
Nutritional Benefits and Cooking for Dietary Needs

HEALTH BENEFITS OF AIR FRYING VS. TRADITIONAL METHODS

The Air Fryer, with its speedy circulation of superheated air around food gives a crisp outside without lots of oil. Many staple foods cooked in UK households fare well in this unique cooking environment:

1. **LESSER FAT CONTENT:** One of the most prominent health benefits of air frying is the reduced fat content in food preparations. Unlike in deep-pan frying that involves high levels of oil and cooking, Air Fryers utilize technology "hot circulation" that creates roughness outside food making it crispy but tender when inside. Therefore, most Air fried products have less than 80% fat compared to their deep-fried counterparts.

2. **LOWER CALORIE CONSUMPTION:** It is also a significant factor as it allows less consumption of calories since not many oils are utilized while Air frying. By cutting out excessive fats from your meals, you can eat your delectable favourites and still stick to your diet of 2800 calories per day.

3. **BETTER NUTRIENT RETENTION:** Air frying retains nutrients greater than boiling and steaming. Vitamin C and other heat-sensitive nutrients get easily broken by high temperatures, but they are kept intact in the case of comparatively low temperature cooking that do not take much time and hence help you avoid overcooked food.

ADAPTING RECIPES TO MEET SPECIFIC DIETARY NEEDS

Another vital trait of a perfect kitchen appliance, Air Fryers are flexible enough for different dietary requirements. Air fryer offers a flexible method of cooking different meals depending on whether you want gluten-free, vegan, or low carb options.

1. **GLUTEN-FREE:** One great way of ensuring one serves healthy meals is by using Air Fryers; it's possible to use different ingredients which have a substitute for flour or bread crumb with no alterations in most recipes. You can use different types of flour blends such as almond flour and substitute any type of flour for gluten-free cereal flakes to give them a similar texture found in popular fried food but with no risk of being contaminated by gluten.

2. **VEGAN:** Air fryer cooking of delicious and healthy vegan dishes has been made easier. Air frying offers an ideal technique of preparing crispy and tasty vegetables including delicious vegan main courses. For instance, one should replace animal protein with options such as tofu or tempeh, use alternatives like almond milk in place of regular milk, and use linseed meal combined with water in place of eggs.

3. **LOW-CARB:** Air frying can be used in preparation of tasty low-carb meals as it allows substitution of other ingredients that are usually excluded due to high level of carbs. By replacing breadcrumbs with pork scratchings, or using coconut flour instead of wheat flour you can have a good crunch without exceeding your carbs count. Then, they can prepare proteins and fats with green leaves and low carbs.

It is usually sufficient to substitute part of the oils in well-known recipes with no further modifications than adjusting Air frying temperatures, settings, and timing in accordance with this models distinctive approach. Remember, every Air fryer brand may have unique specification of operation thus it is necessary to follow directions provided with regard to your own Air Fryer.

HERE IS YOUR FREE GIFT!

- TIPS AND TRICKS
- 30-DAY MEAL PLAN
- WEEKLY SHOPPING LIST

Air Fryer FULL ENGLISH

PREP: 10 min   **COOK:** 20 min   **SERVES:** 4

DIRECTIONS:

1. Warm up your air fryer to 180 degrees Celsius.
2. In your large container, mix bacon, sausages, tomatoes, mushrooms, plus half of oil.
3. Transfer it in your cooking basket. Cook within ten mins. Make four spaces in your cooking basket for your eggs.
4. Put one egg into each space, then drizzle remaining oil. Cook within ten mins.
5. Meanwhile, warm up your baked beans in your saucepan on low temp till warmed. Distribute each portion out on your plate. Serve.

INGREDIENTS:

450 grams rashers of bacon
8 sausages
200 grams cherry tomatoes
250 grams sliced mushrooms
4 big eggs
400 grams baked beans
100 millilitres vegetable oil

NUTRITIONAL VALUES (PER SERVING): CALORIES: 650, CARBS: 32G, FAT: 43G, PROTEIN: 39G

INGREDIENTS:

200 grams bacon rashers
100 grams grated cheddar cheese
4 big eggs
4 English muffins, sliced in half
50 grams unsalted butter, softened
100 millilitres milk
Salt & pepper, as required

Crispy Bacon & EGG MUFFINS

PREP: 10 min   **COOK:** 12 min   **SERVES:** 4

DIRECTIONS:

1. Warm up your air fryer to 180 degrees Celsius. Put bacon rashers on your cooking tray, then cook within six mins till crispy. Put aside.
2. Whisk eggs plus milk in your container, flavour it using salt plus pepper. Pour it into your greased oven-proof dish.
3. Put your oven-proof dish into your air fryer, then cook within six mins.
4. Meanwhile, spread each half of English muffins using butter.
5. Assemble your muffins by putting one half of each muffin on your plate, then layer it with bacon, cooked egg mixture, cheddar, then cover it with another half of your English muffin.

NUTRITIONAL VALUES (PER SERVING): CALORIES: 450, CARBS: 31G, FAT: 26G, PROTEIN: 25G

Sausage & Egg
BREAKFAST ROLLS

🕐 **PREP**: 10 min   📟 **COOK**: 15 min   🍴 **SERVES**: 4

DIRECTIONS:

1. Warm up your air fryer to 180 degrees Celsius. Brush each sausage using oil, then put them in your cooking basket. Cook within ten mins till browned. Put aside.
2. Meanwhile, put eggs into four small containers. Brush your cooking basket using oil, then pour each egg into your basket. Cook within five mins till whites are set.
3. Put two sausages on bottom half of each roll, then add egg on top. Flavour it using salt plus pepper, then close it using top half of each roll. Serve.

INGREDIENTS:

4 bread rolls, halved & toasted
8 pork sausages
4 big eggs
50 millilitres sunflower oil
Salt & pepper, as required

NUTRITIONAL VALUES (PER SERVING): CALORIES: 600, CARBS: 40G, FAT: 37G, PROTEIN: 29G

Egg-in-a-HOLE
TOASTS

🕐 **PREP**: 5 min   📟 **COOK**: 8 min   🍴 **SERVES**: 2

DIRECTIONS:

1. Warm up your air fryer to 180 degrees Celsius. Coad bread slices using oil. Put two bread slices in your cooking basket then cook within two mins.
2. Put egg into each bread hole, then flavour it using salt plus pepper. Cook within six mins till egg white is cooked.
3. Do same with remaining bread slices plus eggs. Serve.

INGREDIENTS:

4 bread slices, sliced hole in each centre
4 big eggs
30 millilitres olive oil
Salt & pepper, as required

NUTRITIONAL VALUES (PER SERVING): CALORIES: 50, CARBS: 36G, FAT: 29G PROTEIN: 25G

Mushroom & Spinach
OMELETTE CUPS

🕐 **PREP**: 10 min　　▣ **COOK**: 15 min　　🍴 **SERVES**: 4

DIRECTIONS:

1. Warm up your air fryer to 180 degrees Celsius.
2. In your container, mix spinach plus mushrooms. Transfer it in your four oiled silicone muffin cups.
3. In another container, whisk eggs, milk, salt plus pepper. Pour it into each silicone cup. Sprinkle cheddar on top.
4. Put filled silicone cups in your cooking basket, then cook within fifteen mins till eggs are set. Serve.

INGREDIENTS:

200 grams spinach, chopped
100 grams mushrooms, sliced
8 big eggs
100 millilitres milk
50 grams cheddar cheese, grated
Salt & pepper, as required
Olive oil spray

NUTRITIONAL VALUES (PER SERVING): CALORIES: 353, CARBS: 6G, FAT: 24G, PROTEIN: 27G

Air Fried
SCOTCH EGGS

🕐 **PREP**: 10 min　　▣ **COOK**: 20 min　　🍴 **SERVES**: 4

DIRECTIONS:

1. Flatten each sausage portion into a thin big round patty. Roll each peeled egg in flour, then put it in your sausage patty centre. Wrap sausage meat around egg.
2. In your small container, beat two eggs plus milk. Dip each covered egg into egg mixture, then roll it in breadcrumbs.
3. Warm up your air fryer to 180 degrees Celsius. Put Scotch eggs in your cooking basket. Cook within Twelve mins till golden, flipping once. Serve.

INGREDIENTS:

450 grams sausage meat, split into four
6 medium eggs, four boiled & peeled, two for coating
100 grams all-purpose flour
200 grams breadcrumbs
50 millilitres milk
Salt & pepper, as required

NUTRITIONAL VALUES (PER SERVING): CALORIES: 675, CARBS: 38G, FAT: 41G, PROTEIN: 35G

Haggis, Neeps, *AND* TATTIE PATTIES

 PREP: *20 min*   COOK: *20 min*   SERVES: *4*

INGREDIENTS:

500 grams haggis
750 grams potatoes (tatties), peeled, diced, boiled, drained & cooled
500 grams turnips (neeps), peeled, diced, boiled, drained & cooled
30 millilitres olive oil
Salt & pepper, as required

DIRECTIONS:

1. Warm up your air fryer to 180 degrees Celsius.
2. In your big container, mash potatoes, turnips, plus haggis. Flavour it using salt plus pepper. Shape it into eight patties, then brush them using oil.
3. Put them in your cooking basket. Cook within twenty mins, flipping once. Serve.

NUTRITIONAL VALUES (PER SERVING): CALORIES: 560, CARBS: 62G, FAT: 23G, PROTEIN: 24G

INGREDIENTS:

500 grams potatoes, peeled, grated & squeezed moisture
50 grams cheddar cheese, grated
30 millilitres olive oil
15 grams chives, chopped
Salt & pepper, as required

Hash Browns *WITH* CHEESE AND CHIVES

 PREP: *10 min*   COOK: *20 min*   SERVES: *4*

DIRECTIONS:

1. Warm up your air fryer to 200 degrees Celsius.
2. In your container, mix potatoes, cheddar, oil, chives, salt plus pepper. Form it into eight hash brown patty.
3. Transfer them in your cooking basket. Cook within ten mins per side, then flip each patty. Cook within ten mins till crispy. Serve.

NUTRITIONAL VALUES (PER SERVING): CALORIES 283, CARBS 27G, FAT 16G, PROTEIN 9G

Crispy Air FRYER KIPPERS

🕐 **PREP:** 10 min   🍲 **COOK:** 15 min   🍴 **SERVES:** 4

DIRECTIONS:

1. Warm up your air fryer to 180 degrees Celsius. Brush kippers using lemon juice, then put aside.
2. In your small container, mix flour, pepper, paprika, plus sea salt. Coat each kipper with it. Drizzle oil on each kipper.
3. Put them in your cooking basket, then cook within fifteen mins till crispy, flipping once. Serve.

INGREDIENTS:

4 (150 grams each) kippers, washed & pat dried
30 millilitres lemon juice
30 grams plain flour
Three grams black pepper
Three grams paprika
Three grams sea salt
20 millilitres vegetable oil

NUTRITIONAL VALUES (PER SERVING): CALORIES: 260, CARBS: 6G, FAT: 13G, PROTEIN: 29G

INGREDIENTS:

500 grams trimmed asparagus spears
400 grams streaky bacon
15 millilitres olive oil
Salt & black pepper, as required

Bacon Wrapped ASPARAGUS SPEARS

🕐 **PREP:** 10 min   🍲 **COOK:** 10 min   🍴 **SERVES:** 4

DIRECTIONS:

1. Warm up your air fryer to 200 degrees Celsius. Lay out bacon on your clean surface.
2. Toss asparagus spears plus oil. Flavour asparagus using salt plus black pepper. Wrap one bacon strip around each asparagus spear.
3. Put them in your cooking basket. Cook within ten mins till bacon is crispy. Serve.

NUTRITIONAL VALUES (PER SERVING): CALORIES: 280, CARBS: 5G, FAT: 22G, PROTEIN: 18G

Cheesy Beans
ON TOASTED CRUMPETS

🕐 **PREP**: 10 min   📟 **COOK**: 15 min   🍴 **SERVES**: 4

DIRECTIONS:

1. Warm up your air fryer to 190 degrees Celsius.
2. In your small container, mix baked beans plus milk. Put crumpets in your cooking basket, then brush them using butter on top.
3. Cook within three to five mins till lightly crisp. Put aside.
4. Spoon bean mixture on top of each crumpet. Sprinkle Cheddar on each bean-topped crumpet.
5. Put loaded crumpets to your cooking basket, then cook within six to eight mins till cheese is melted. Serve.

INGREDIENTS:

Eight (350 grams) crumpets
200 grams grated Cheddar cheese
400 grams canned baked beans in tomato sauce
50 millilitres whole milk
20 grams salted butter, dissolved

NUTRITIONAL VALUES (PER SERVING): CALORIES: 520, CARBS: 60G, FAT: 22G, PROTEIN: 23G

Welsh RAREBIT
BITES

🕐 **PREP**: 15 min   📟 **COOK**: 8 min   🍴 **SERVES**: 4

DIRECTIONS:

1. Warm up your air fryer to 180 degrees Celsius.
2. In your container, mix cheese, butter, Worcestershire, and English mustard. Add egg plus black pepper, then mix again.
3. Spread it onto your bread cubes. Put coated bread cubes in your cooking basket. Cook within six to eight mins till crispy. Serve.

INGREDIENTS:

200 grams whole-wheat bread, sliced into bite-sized cubes
150 grams sharp cheddar cheese, grated
50 grams unsalted butter, softened
30 millilitres Worcestershire sauce
Ten millilitres English mustard
One big egg, beaten
Ground black pepper, as required

NUTRITIONAL VALUES (PER SERVING): CALORIES: 400, CARBS: 23G, FAT: 30G, PROTEIN: 16G

Egg & Bacon
BREAKFAST BURRITOS

🕐 **PREP**: 10 min   🍲 **COOK**: 15 min   🍴 **SERVES**: 4

DIRECTIONS:

1. Warm up your air fryer to 180 degrees Celsius. In your container, whisk eggs, milk, salt, plus pepper.
2. Cook bacon slices in your air fryer within five mins till crisp. Put aside.
3. Scramble egg mixture in your pan on moderate temp till firm.
4. Lay out each tortilla wrap, then split scrambled eggs, bacon, cheddar, plus tomatoes among them. Roll up each tortilla tightly.
5. Put burritos into your cooking basket, then cook within seven mins till crispy. Serve.

INGREDIENTS:

Four big eggs
Eight rashers of bacon
Four whole-wheat tortilla wraps
100 grams grated cheddar cheese
50 grams diced tomatoes
30 millilitres milk
Salt & pepper, as required

NUTRITIONAL VALUES (PER SERVING): CALORIES: 472, CARBS: 32G, FAT: 27G, PROTEIN: 29G

Sausage, Egg & CHEESE
BREAKFAST SANDWICH

🕐 **PREP**: 10 min   🍲 **COOK**: 15 min   🍴 **SERVES**: 4

DIRECTIONS:

1. Warm up your air fryer to 180 degrees Celsius. Form sausage meat into four patties.
2. Put them in your cooking basket, then cook within ten mins, flipping once.
3. Meanwhile, whisk eggs, milk, salt plus pepper.
4. Pour it into your oiled pan on moderate temp, then cook till scrambled.
5. Remove cooked sausage patties, then put a cheese slice on each patty. Let it melt.
6. Toast English muffins in your cooking basket within two mins.
7. Put one sausage patty plus scrambled eggs onto each English muffin bottom half, then top using other half of your muffin.

INGREDIENTS:

250 grams sausage meat
100 grams cheddar cheese, grated
Four eggs
100 millilitres milk
Salt & pepper, as required
Four English muffins, split

NUTRITIONAL VALUES (PER SERVING): CALORIES: 600, CARBS: 36G, FAT: 37G, PROTEIN: 29G

Blueberry & Cream
CHEESE PASTRIES

🕐 **PREP**: 15 min   🍲 **COOK**: 20 min   🍴 **SERVES**: 6

DIRECTIONS:
1. Warm up your air fryer to 180 degrees Celsius. Roll out puff pastry on your floured surface, then slice it into six squares.
2. In your container, mix cream cheese, sugar, egg yolk, plus vanilla till smooth.
3. Put cream cheese mixture into each puff pastry square centre. Top each with blueberries.
4. Fold corners of each pastry square inwards, then pinch them to seal.
5. Put them in your cooking basket. Cook within twenty mins till pastries are golden. Serve.

INGREDIENTS:

200 grams puff pastry
120 grams cream cheese, softened
60 grams granulated sugar
One egg yolk
Five millilitres vanilla extract
200 grams fresh blueberries

NUTRITIONAL VALUES (PER SERVING): CALORIES: 350, CARBS: 34G, FAT: 21G, PROTEIN: 6G

INGREDIENTS:

220 grams all-purpose flour
1.5 grams salt
50 grams unsalted butter, cubed and chilled
150 millilitres milk
15 grams caster sugar
Ten grams baking powder
Clotted cream & jam, for serving

Air Fried SCONES WITH
CLOTTED CREAM & JAM

🕐 **PREP**: 15 min   🍲 **COOK**: 10 min   🍴 **SERVES**: 8

DIRECTIONS:

1. In your big container, mix flour, salt, plus baking powder. Add butter, then mix till crumbly. Mix in sugar.
2. Pour milk, mixing gently till a soft dough form. Lightly flour your work surface, then gently knead your dough within thirty seconds.
3. Roll out your dough to two centimetres thick. Slice out eight scones from your dough.
4. Warm up your air fryer to 200 degrees Celsius. Put scones onto your lined cooking basket.
5. Cook within ten mins till golden brown. Cool it down, then serve. Serve with clotted cream plus jam on top.

NUTRITIONAL VALUES (PER SERVING): CALORIES: 185, CARBS: 28G, FAT: 6G, PROTEIN: 4G

Cinnamon
& RAISIN BAGELS

🕐 PREP: *20 min*   🍲 COOK: *12 min*   🍴 SERVES: *6*

DIRECTIONS:

1. In your big container, mix flour, yeast, granulated sugar, plus salt. Mix in warm water till a dough forms.
2. Knead within ten mins till it becomes elastic. Add raisins plus cinnamon, then knead within two mins. Split dough into six, then shape them into balls.
3. Create a hole in each ball centre using your thumb till a bagel shape form.
4. Warm up your air fryer to 180 degrees Celsius. Coat your cooking basket using oil.
5. Put three bagels into your cooking basket, then cook within six mins. Flip them, then cook within six mins till golden brown. Cool it down. Do same for rest of bagels. Serve.

INGREDIENTS:

360 grams plain flour
One sachet (seven grams) instant yeast
30 grams granulated sugar
240 millilitres warm water
Five grams salt
Five millilitres vegetable oil
150 grams raisins
Five grams ground cinnamon

NUTRITIONAL VALUES (PER SERVING): CALORIES: 350, CARBS: 72G, FAT: 1.5G, PROTEIN: 9G

INGREDIENTS:

500 grams bacon strips
60 millilitres maple syrup
Five grams black pepper
Five grams paprika

Maple-Glazed BACON
STRIPS

🕐 PREP: *10 min*   🍲 COOK: *10 min*   🍴 SERVES: *4*

DIRECTIONS:

1. Warm up your air fryer to 180 degrees Celsius.
2. In your shallow container, mix maple syrup, pepper, plus paprika. Dip each bacon strip into it.
3. Put coated bacon strips in your cooking basket. Cook within five mins, then flip them. Cook within three to five mins till crispy. Cool it down, then serve.

NUTRITIONAL VALUES (PER SERVING): CALORIES: 490, CARBS: 12G, FAT: 40G, PROTEIN: 19G

Egg & Chorizo
BREAKFAST TACOS

🕐 **PREP:** 10 min   🍳 **COOK:** 12 min   🍴 **SERVES:** 4

DIRECTIONS:

1. Warm up your air fryer to 180 degrees Celsius.
2. In your container, mix baby potatoes, chorizo, salt plus pepper. Put it into your cooking basket, then cook within six mins.
3. Meanwhile, whisk eggs plus milk in your container.
4. Mix potato-chorizo mixture in your cooking basket, then pour egg mixture on it. Cook within four to six mins till cooked.
5. Split egg-chorizo filling among your tortillas. Top each taco using cheddar cheese plus your choice of salsa and toppings.

INGREDIENTS:

300g baby potatoes, diced
150g uncooked chorizo, diced
Eight big eggs, beaten
50ml whole milk
Salt & pepper, as required
Eight small corn tortillas, warmed
100g cheddar cheese, grated
Salsa & toppings of choice

NUTRITIONAL VALUES (PER SERVING): CALORIES: 575, CARBS: 38G, FAT: 34G, PROTEIN: 30G

Smoked Salmon
& CREAM CHEESE BAGEL BITES

🕐 **PREP:** 10 min   🍳 **COOK:** 6 min   🍴 **SERVES:** 4

DIRECTIONS:

1. Warm up your air fryer to 180 degrees Celsius.
2. In your small container, mix cream cheese plus lemon juice till smooth. Coat bagels using olive oil.
3. Put bagel pieces in your cooking basket, then cook within three mins, then flip them. Cook within three mins till crispy.
4. Cool them down before topping them using cream cheese mixture. Put smoked salmon slice on top. Flavour it using salt plus pepper. Serve.

INGREDIENTS:

120 grams smoked salmon, sliced
100 grams cream cheese, softened
Four plain bagels, sliced into bite-sized pieces
30 millilitres olive oil
15 millilitres lemon juice
Salt & pepper, as required

NUTRITIONAL VALUES (PER SERVING): CALORIES: 610, CARBS: 68G, FAT: 24G, PROTEIN: 35G

Stuffed French
TOAST WITH BERRIES

🕐 **PREP**: 10 min   🍳 **COOK**: 8 min   🍴 **SERVES**: 4

DIRECTIONS:

1. In your small container, mix cream cheese plus raspberry jam. Fill each bread pocket using cream cheese-berry mixture.
2. In your shallow container, whisk eggs, milk, cinnamon, plus vanilla. Warm up your air fryer to 180 degrees Celsius.
3. Dip each stuffed bread into your egg mixture. Put coated stuffed bread in your oiled cooking basket.
4. Cook within four mins per side, till crispy. Cool it down, then dust with powdered sugar. Serve.

INGREDIENTS:

200 grams thick-sliced bread, sliced in four & sliced a pocket in each
100 grams cream cheese
50 grams raspberry jam
200 grams mixed berries
Two big eggs
60 millilitres whole milk
Five grams ground cinnamon
Five grams vanilla extract
20 grams powdered sugar (for dusting)

NUTRITIONAL VALUES (PER SERVING): CALORIES: 390, CARBS: 49G, FAT: 18G, PROTEIN: 12G

INGREDIENTS:

180 grams flour, self-raising
120 grams applesauce, unsweetened
100 grams chocolate chips
60 grams sugar, granulated
60 millilitres each vegetable oil & whole milk
Three big eggs

Chocolate Chip
BREAKFAST MUFFINS

🕐 **PREP**: 15 min   🍳 **COOK**: 12 min   🍴 **SERVES**: 6

DIRECTIONS:

1. In your big container, whisk eggs, sugar, oil, plus milk. Fold in flour, then mix till smooth. Mix in apple sauce plus chocolate chips.
2. Warm up your air fryer to 180 degrees Celsius. Spoon batter into your silicone muffin tray.
3. Put muffin tray or cups in your cooking basket, then cook within twelve mins till firm. Remove, cool it down, then serve.

NUTRITIONAL VALUES (PER SERVING): CALORIES: 365, CARBS: 46G, FAT: 18G, PROTEIN: 8G

Plum & Almond
BREAKFAST TARTS

 PREP: *12 min*   **COOK**: *10 min*   **SERVES**: *6*

DIRECTIONS:

1. In your big container, mix flour plus butter till crumbly.
2. Slowly add ice water, mixing till dough comes together. Knead within one min, then form dough into a ball. Wrap in cling film, then refrigerate within fifteen mins.
3. Meanwhile, in your separate container, mix ground almonds, caster sugar, almond extract, eggs, plus double cream.
4. Warm up your air fryer to 180 degrees Celsius. Lightly oil your six tart tins.
5. Take chilled dough, then roll it out on your lightly floured surface. Slice out six dough circles slightly larger than your tart tins. Press dough circles into your tins.
6. Spoon almond mixture between your six tart shells. Arrange plum slices on top.
7. Put tarts into your cooking basket, then cook within ten mins till set. Cool it down, then serve.

INGREDIENTS:

300 grams all-purpose flour
150 grams cold unsalted butter, cubed
50 millilitres ice water
200 grams plums, pitted & sliced
100 grams almonds, ground
75 grams caster sugar
30 millilitres almond extract
Two big eggs
100 millilitres double cream

NUTRITIONAL VALUES (PER SERVING): CALORIES: 490, CARBS: 47G, FAT: 29G, PROTEIN: 10G

Crispy
FISH GOUJONS

🕐 **PREP**: 15 min   🍲 **COOK**: 10 min   🍴 **SERVES**: 4

DIRECTIONS:

1. In your shallow container, mix flour, salt, plus pepper. In another shallow container, whisk eggs. In your third shallow container, add breadcrumbs.
2. Dredge each fish goujon in flour mixture, dip it in egg wash, then coat it using breadcrumbs.
3. Warm up your air fryer to 200 degrees Celsius. Coat crumbed fish goujons using oil, then put them in your cooking basket.
4. Cook within ten mins crispy, flipping once. Serve.

INGREDIENTS:

500 grams white fish fillets, pat dried & sliced into strips
100 grams plain flour
Salt & black pepper, as required
Two big eggs
200 grams breadcrumbs
50 millilitres vegetable oil

NUTRITIONAL VALUES (PER SERVING): CALORIES: 460, CARBS: 52G, FAT: 15G, PROTEIN: 32G

Mini Cheese & ONION
PASTIES

🕐 **PREP**: 15 min   🍲 **COOK**: 10 min   🍴 **SERVES**: 6

DIRECTIONS:

1. In your container, mix cheese, onion, parsley, salt plus pepper.
2. Roll out puff pastry on your lightly floured surface. Slice out twelve circles from your puff pastry.
3. Put 15g cheese-onion mixture in six pastry circles. Brush edges some water, then put another circle on top to form a pasty, pressing edges to seal.
4. Warm up your air fryer to 180 degrees Celsius. Brush each pasty using egg wash.
5. Put mini cheese-onion pasties in your cooking basket, then cook within ten mins till puffed up. Serve.

INGREDIENTS:

200 grams puff pastry
100 grams cheddar cheese, grated
150 grams onion, chopped
Seven grams parsley, chopped
Salt & pepper, as required
One egg, beaten
Flour for dusting

NUTRITIONAL VALUES (PER SERVING): CALORIES: 310, CARBS: 24G, FAT: 20G, PROTEIN: 9G

Crispy
CHICKEN NUGGETS

🕐 **PREP**: 15 min   📱 **COOK**: 12 min   🍴 **SERVES**: 4

DIRECTIONS:

1. Prepare three shallow containers. Mix flour, salt, plus pepper in first, put breadcrumbs in second, then beat eggs in third.
2. Dip each chicken cube into flour mixture, then into eggs, then coat them into breadcrumbs.
3. Warm up your air fryer to 200 degrees Celsius. Put chicken nuggets in your oiled cooking basket, then spray them using oil.
4. Cook within six mins, then flip them. Cook within six mins till golden brown. Cool it down, then serve.

INGREDIENTS:

500 grams no bones & skin chicken breasts, cubed
100 grams flour, all-purpose
Salt & black pepper, as required
200 grams panko breadcrumbs
Two big eggs, beaten
30 millilitres olive oil

NUTRITIONAL VALUES (PER SERVING): CALORIES: 412, CARBS: 41G, FAT: 12G, PROTEIN: 34G

Sticky BBQ
CHICKEN WINGS

🕐 **PREP**: 15 min   📱 **COOK**: 20 min   🍴 **SERVES**: 4

DIRECTIONS:

1. In your big container, mix BBQ sauce, honey, paprika, powdered garlic, salt, plus pepper.
2. Add chicken wings, then toss them till coated. Marinate within one hour in your fridge.
3. Warm up your air fryer to 200 degrees Celsius. Toss wings in oil till coated.
4. Put wings in your cooking basket. Cook within twenty-five mins, flipping them once. Serve.

INGREDIENTS:

One kilogram chicken wings
200 millilitres BBQ sauce
50 grams honey
Two grams paprika
Two grams powdered garlic
Salt & pepper, as required
30 millilitres vegetable oil

NUTRITIONAL VALUES (PER SERVING): CALORIES: 520, CARBS: 32G, FAT: 31G, PROTEIN: 31G

Cumberland
SAUSAGE ROLLS

🕐 **PREP**: 15 min   🍲 **COOK**: 12 min   🍴 **SERVES**: 4

DIRECTIONS:

1. Warm up your air fryer to 200 degrees Celsius.
2. In your container, mix Cumberland sausages plus cooked onions.
3. Flour your work surface, then unroll your puff pastry sheet. Slice puff pastry into four rectangles.
4. Put quarter sausage mixture on each rectangle, then form it into a line along one long edge of your pastry.
5. Brush other long edge of your pastry with beaten egg. Roll up each rectangle to create four long rolls, pressing to seal.
6. Brush tops using more beaten egg. Transfer sausage rolls to your cooking basket. Cook within twelve mins till golden brown.

INGREDIENTS:

400 grams Cumberland sausages
320 grams puff pastry sheet (one ready-rolled sheet)
100 grams cooked & cooled onions, chopped
50 millilitres beaten egg
Flour, for dusting

NUTRITIONAL VALUES (PER SERVING): CALORIES: 672, CARBS: 44G, FAT: 47G, PROTEIN: 22G

INGREDIENTS:

100 grams plain flour
Two eggs
150 millilitres milk
Salt & black pepper, as required
50 millilitres vegetable oil
300 grams roast beef slices, cooked & thinly sliced
40 grams horseradish sauce

Mini Yorkshire
Puddings WITH ROAST BEEF & HORSERADISH

🕐 **PREP**: 10 min   🍲 **COOK**: 15 min   🍴 **SERVES**: 4

DIRECTIONS:

1. In your big container, mix flour, eggs, plus milk till smooth, then flavour it using salt plus black pepper.
2. Warm up your air fryer to 200 degrees Celsius. Pour oil into each air fryer-safe mini muffin tin cavity.
3. Put tin in your cooking basket, then cook within two to three mins. Remove hot tin, then fill each oiled cavity with batter.
4. Cook within fifteen mins till puddings are puffed. Remove, then cool it down.
5. To serve, top each pudding using roast beef slice plus horseradish sauce. Serve.

NUTRITIONAL VALUES (PER SERVING): CALORIES: 425, CARBS: 28G, FAT: 21G, PROTEIN: 32G

Air Fried
BLACK PUDDING SLICES

🕐 **PREP**: 5 min   📠 **COOK**: 12 min   🍴 **SERVES**: 4

DIRECTIONS:

1. Warm up your air fryer to 200 degrees Celsius.
2. In your container, mix black pudding slices, oil, salt, plus pepper.
3. Put coated black pudding slices in your cooking basket. Cook within six mins, then flip them. Cook within six mins till crispy. Serve.

INGREDIENTS:

500 grams black pudding, sliced into one cm thick pieces
30 millilitres olive oil
Salt & pepper, as required

NUTRITIONAL VALUES (PER SERVING): CALORIES 374, CARBS 2G, FAT 33G, PROTEIN 16G

INGREDIENTS:

Four sourdough bread slices
100 grams mature Cheddar cheese, grated
50 millilitres milk
25 grams butter
15 grams all-purpose flour
15 millilitres Worcestershire sauce
One egg, beaten
Five millilitres Dijon mustard

Welsh
RAREBIT TOASTIES

🕐 **PREP**: 10 min   📠 **COOK**: 8 min   🍴 **SERVES**: 4

DIRECTIONS:

1. In your small saucepan, dissolve butter on moderate temp. Add flour, mixing within one min.
2. Gradually add milk, mixing till smooth.
3. Remove saucepan, then mix in cheese, Worcestershire, plus mustard. Cool slightly, then mix in beaten egg.
4. Warm up your air fryer to 180 degrees Celsius. Lightly oil your cooking basket.
5. Spread cheese mixture onto each sourdough bread slice.
6. Put two bread slices with cheese mixture facing up into your cooking basket.
7. Cook within six to eight mins till crispy. Repeat using rest of slices. Remove, cool it down, slice, then serve.

NUTRITIONAL VALUES (PER SERVING): CALORIES: 384, CARBS: 28G, FAT: 23G, PROTEIN: 16G

Pork Pie
BITES WITH PICKLE

🕐 **PREP**: 20 min   🍲 **COOK**: 25 min   🍴 **SERVES**: 4

DIRECTIONS:

1. In your big container, mix flour plus butter till crumbly.
2. In your small saucepan, warm up lard plus water till melted. Pour it into flour-butter mixture. Mix till a dough forms.
3. Roll out dough on your lightly floured surface. Slice out twelve dough circles. Warm up your air fryer to 180 degrees Celsius.
4. Press dough circles into your mini muffin tin cups.
5. In another container, mix pork shoulder, pickle, salt, plus pepper.
6. Spoon some pork mixture into each pie crust. Fold excess dough over your filling to create a sealed top. Brush each pie bite using beaten egg.
7. Put filled muffin tin in your cooking basket, then cook within twenty-five mins till golden brown.

INGREDIENTS:

500 grams pork shoulder, minced
150 grams flour, all-purpose
75 grams butter, cold and cubed
50 grams lard
100 millilitres water
One egg, lightly beaten
120 millilitres pickle (of your choice), diced
Salt & pepper, as required

NUTRITIONAL VALUES (PER SERVING): CALORIES 390; CARBS 23G; FAT 24G; PROTEIN 18G

Stilton & BROCCOLI
SOUP SHOOTERS

🕐 **PREP**: 15 min   🍲 **COOK**: 20 min   🍴 **SERVES**: 6

DIRECTIONS:

1. Warm up your air fryer to 180 degrees Celsius.
2. Toss broccoli plus oil, then put them in your cooking basket. Cook within ten mins till slightly charred, shaking once.
3. In your big saucepan, warm up broth, then let it boil. Add cooked broccoli, then simmer within five mins.
4. Turn off its heat, add Stilton cheese, then mix till melted. Blend soup using your immersion blender till smooth. Mix in heavy cream, salt plus pepper. Serve into shot glasses.

INGREDIENTS:

500 grams broccoli florets
250 grams Stilton cheese, crumbled
One litre vegetable broth
150 millilitres heavy cream
30 millilitres olive oil
Salt & pepper, as required

NUTRITIONAL VALUES (PER SERVING): CALORIES: 333; CARBS: 6G; FAT: 28G; PROTEIN: 14G

Battered Mushy
PEA FRITTERS

🕐 **PREP**: 15 min   📷 **COOK**: 20 min   🍴 **SERVES**: 4

DIRECTIONS:

1. Warm up your air fryer to 180 degrees Celsius.
2. In your container, mix flour plus cold water till smooth. Mix in mushy peas plus salt. Form it into fritter, then transfer them in your cooking basket.
3. Cook within ten mins, then flip them. Cook within ten mins till crisp.
4. Put potato chips in your cooking basket. Cook within twenty mins till crispy, shaking once. Serve mushy pea fritters with chips.

INGREDIENTS:

400 grams mushy peas
150 grams flour, self-raising
200 millilitres cold water
One-kilogram potatoes, peeled & sliced into thick chips
Salt, as required
Cooking spray

NUTRITIONAL VALUES (PER SERVING): CALORIES: 425, CARBS: 67G, FAT: 11G, PROTEIN: 14G

Mini
CORNISH PASTIES

🕐 **PREP**: 15 min   📷 **COOK**: 20 min   🍴 **SERVES**: 4

DIRECTIONS:

1. In your big container, mix flour plus butter till crumbly.
2. Add cold water, then mix till it forms a dough. Wrap dough, then refrigerate within thirty mins.
3. Mix potatoes, swede, onion, skirt steak, salt, plus pepper in another container. Flavour it using salt plus pepper to taste.
4. Warm up your air fryer to 180 degrees Celsius.
5. On your floured surface, roll out dough to about three millimetres thickness. Slice twelve circles of dough.
6. Spoon filling onto each circle of dough, fold, then crimp edges. Brush each pasty with beaten egg, then transfer them to your cooking basket.
7. Cook within twenty mins till golden brown. Serve.

INGREDIENTS:

200 grams plain flour
100 grams cold unsalted butter, diced
60 millilitres cold water
150 grams potatoes, peeled & diced
100 grams swede, peeled & diced
80 grams onion, chopped
150 grams skirt steak, sliced
Salt & pepper, as required
One egg, beaten

NUTRITIONAL VALUES (PER SERVING): CALORIES: 580, CARBS: 60G, FAT: 30G, PROTEIN: 25G

Bacon-Wrapped
DATES WITH BLUE CHEESE

🕐 **PREP**: 15 min　　📠 **COOK**: 10 min　　🍴 **SERVES**: 4

DIRECTIONS:

1. Warm up your air fryer to 180 degrees Celsius.
2. Stuff each date with blue cheese. Wrap each stuffed date using half bacon slice.
3. Coat your cooking basket using oil.
4. Put bacon-wrapped dates in your cooking basket. Cook within ten mins till the bacon is crispy. Remove, cool it down, then serve.

INGREDIENTS:

Twenty-four dates, slitted & pitted
Twelve bacon rashers, sliced in half
100 grams blue cheese, crumbled
15 millilitres Olive oil

NUTRITIONAL VALUES (PER SERVING): CALORIES: 390, CARBS: 30G, FAT: 22G, PROTEIN: 18G

Mini Toad
IN THE HOLE

🕐 **PREP**: 15 min　　📠 **COOK**: 20 min　　🍴 **SERVES**: 4

DIRECTIONS:

1. In your big container, mix flour, milk, eggs, plus salt till smooth. Put aside.
2. Warm up your air fryer to 200 degrees Celsius. Put browned sausages in your oiled cooking basket. Pour batter on sausages.
3. Cook within twenty mins till golden. Serve.

INGREDIENTS:

150 grams plain flour
300 millilitres milk
Two big eggs
Salt, as required
Twelve small pork sausages, browned
15 millilitres vegetable oil

NUTRITIONAL VALUES (PER SERVING): CALORIES: 615, CARBS: 40G, FAT: 36G, PROTEIN: 29G

Spicy Chicken
SATAY SKEWERS

🕐 **PREP**: 15 min   📠 **COOK**: 10 min   🍴 **SERVES**: 4

DIRECTIONS:

1. In your container, mix peanut butter, soy sauce, sweet chili sauce, juice, oil, plus coriander.
2. Add chicken strips, then refrigerate within one hour. Warm up your air fryer to 180 degrees Celsius.
3. Thread marinated chicken onto your soaked bamboo skewers. Put skewers in your cooking basket, then cook within five mins.
4. Flip them, then cook within five mins till cooked. Serve.

INGREDIENTS:

500 grams no bones & skin chicken breasts, thin strips
100 grams crunchy peanut butter
60 millilitres soy sauce
30 millilitres sweet chili sauce
20 millilitres lime juice
10 millilitres vegetable oil
10 grams ground coriander

NUTRITIONAL VALUES (PER SERVING): CALORIES: 410, CARBS: 11G, FAT: 26G, PROTEIN: 36G

INGREDIENTS:

200 grams Camembert cheese, wedges
50g flour, all-purpose
100 grams breadcrumbs
Two eggs, beaten
150 millilitres cranberry sauce

Breaded Camembert
WITH CRANBERRY SAUCE

🕐 **PREP**: 10 min   📠 **COOK**: 8 min   🍴 **SERVES**: 4

DIRECTIONS:

1. Warm up your air fryer to 180 degrees Celsius.
2. Put flour, beaten eggs, and breadcrumbs in separate shallow container.
3. Coat each Camembert wedge using flour, in egg, then in breadcrumbs, pressing.
4. Put breaded Camembert wedges in your cooking basket. Cook within eight mins till crisp.
5. Meanwhile, warm up cranberry sauce in your small saucepan on low temp in your microwave within one min.
6. Serve breaded Camembert wedges with cranberry sauce for dipping.

NUTRITIONAL VALUES (PER SERVING): CALORIES: 384, CARBS: 30G, FAT: 22G, PROTEIN: 17G

Smoked Mackerel Pâté
ON TOASTED CROUTONS

🕐 **PREP**: 15 min   🍲 **COOK**: 10 min   🍴 **SERVES**: 4

DIRECTIONS:

1. In your food processor, mix smoked mackerel, cream cheese, double cream, plus juice. Blend till smooth.
2. Flavour it using salt plus pepper. Transfer it to your container, then refrigerate for a while.
3. Warm up your air fryer to 180 degrees Celsius. Put bread squares evenly in your cooking basket.
4. Cook within five mins till crispy. Remove, then cool it down. Spread some smoked mackerel pâté onto each toasted crouton. Serve.

INGREDIENTS:

200 grams smoked mackerel, skin removed
100 grams cream cheese
50 millilitres double cream
Juice of half a lemon
Eight wholegrain bread slices, sliced into crouton-sized squares
Salt & pepper, as required

NUTRITIONAL VALUES (PER SERVING): CALORIES: 463, CARBS: 32G, FAT: 26G, PROTEIN: 27G

Corned Beef
& PICKLE SANDWICHES

🕐 PREP: 10 min   🍲 COOK: 4 min   SERVES: 4

DIRECTIONS:

1. Warm up your air fryer to 180 degrees Celsius.
2. Spread one side of each bread slice using butter. Layer corned beef plus pickles in your four bread slices.
3. Drizzle each with five millilitres English mustard, then top with rocket leaves. Put remaining bread slices on top.
4. Put sandwiches in your cooking basket, then cook within two mins per side or till crispy. Serve.

INGREDIENTS:

400 grams corned beef, sliced
Eight wholemeal bread slices
100 grams pickles, sliced
50 grams unsalted butter, softened
20 millilitres English mustard
50 grams rocket leaves

NUTRITIONAL VALUES (PER SERVING): CALORIES: 526, CARBS: 58G, FAT: 23G, PROTEIN: 36G

Cottage Pie Stuffed
JACKET POTATOES

🕐 PREP: 15 min   🍲 COOK: 45 min   SERVES: 4

DIRECTIONS:

1. Warm up your air fryer to 180 degrees Celsius.
2. Put potatoes in your cooking basket, then cook within forty-five mins till tender, flipping once.
3. Meanwhile, warm up your big non-stick pan on moderate temp. Add beef, then cook till browned, breaking it up.
4. Add onion plus garlic, then cook within five mins till softened. Mix in vegetables, plus beef stock. Let it boil, then simmer within ten mins. Remove, then cool it down.
5. Slice each potato in half lengthways, then scoop out potato flesh into your big container.
6. Mash potato flesh with milk, salt plus pepper. Mix in half of cheese.
7. Fill each hollowed-out potato-half with a beef filling layer, then top using mashed potato mixture.
8. Put filled potatoes back into your cooking basket, then top using rest of grated cheese.
9. Cook within five to ten mins till cheese is melted. Serve.

INGREDIENTS:

Four big baking potatoes, pricked all over
400 grams lean minced beef
150 grams frozen mixed vegetables (peas, carrots, and corn)
120 grams chopped onion
Two cloves garlic, minced
200 millilitres beef stock
100 millilitres milk
50 grams grated cheddar cheese
Salt & pepper, as required

NUTRITIONAL VALUES (PER SERVING): CALORIES: 514, CARBS: 56G, FAT: 17G, PROTEIN: 29G

Crispy Fish Finger
SANDWICH WITH TARTARE SAUCE

🕐 **PREP**: 15 min   📠 **COOK**: 10 min   🍴 **SERVES**: 4

DIRECTIONS:

1. Warm up your air fryer to 200 degrees Celsius.
2. In three separate shallow containers, put flour, beaten egg, plus breadcrumbs. Flavour flour using salt plus pepper.
3. Coat each fish finger in flour, dip in beaten egg, then cover using breadcrumbs. Spray your cooking basket using oil.
4. Put breaded fish fingers into your cooking basket. Spray on top with oil. Cook within ten mins till golden brown.
5. Spread tartare sauce on bread slice, adding two crispy fish fingers on top, then covering with another bread slice. Serve.

INGREDIENTS:

400 grams white fish fillets, sliced into sticks
50 grams plain flour
One egg, beaten
100 grams breadcrumbs
100 grams tartare sauce
Eight slices bread
Two litres vegetable oil, for spraying
Salt & pepper, as required

NUTRITIONAL VALUES (PER SERVING): CALORIES: 629, CARBS: 59G, FAT: 27G, PROTEIN: 37G

Coronation Chicken
SALAD WRAPS

🕐 **PREP**: 15 min   📠 **COOK**: 12 min   🍴 **SERVES**: 4

INGREDIENTS:

400 grams no bones & skin chicken breasts
50 millilitres Greek yogurt
50 millilitres mayonnaise
Ten grams curry powder
20 grams mango chutney
Five grams ground turmeric
Salt & pepper, as required
100 grams mixed salad greens
Four big tortilla wraps

DIRECTIONS:

1. Warm up your air fryer to 200 degrees Celsius.
2. Flavour chicken breasts using salt, pepper, plus turmeric.
3. Put seasoned chicken breasts in your cooking basket, then cook within twelve mins, turning once till fully cooked. Remove, cool it down, then slice into thin strips.
4. Meanwhile, mix yogurt, mayonnaise, curry powder, plus mango chutney in your container. Put aside.
5. Lay out each tortilla wrap on your flat surface, then spread some coronation sauce on each wrap.
6. Divide mixed salad greens among your four wraps, then top using sliced chicken.
7. Roll up each tortilla wrap, then slice in half diagonally. Serve.

NUTRITIONAL VALUES (PER SERVING): CALORIES: 415, CARBS: 40G, FAT: 13G, PROTEIN: 36G

Bubble &
SQUEAK CAKES

🕐 **PREP**: 15 min   📦 **COOK**: 25 min   🍴 **SERVES**: 4

DIRECTIONS:

1. In your big container, mix potatoes, Brussels sprouts, carrots, plus onions. Flavour it using salt plus pepper. Mix in flour, plus eggs. Shape it into eight patty cakes. Brush each cake using oil.
2. Warm up your air fryer to 200 degrees Celsius. Put four cakes into your cooking basket.
3. Cook within ten mins, then flip them. Cook within ten mins till crispy. Do same using rest of patty cakes. Serve.

INGREDIENTS:

400 grams cooked potatoes, mashed
300 grams cooked Brussels sprouts, chopped
100 grams cooked carrots, chopped
80 grams onion, chopped
50 grams flour, all-purpose
Two big eggs, beaten
30 millilitres olive oil
Salt & pepper, as required

NUTRITIONAL VALUES (PER SERVING): CALORIES: 320, CARBS: 40G, FAT: 12G, PROTEIN: 10G

Bangers &
MASH SLIDERS

🕐 **PREP**: 15 min   📦 **COOK**: 30 min   🍴 **SERVES**: 4

DIRECTIONS:

1. Warm up your air fryer to 180 degrees Celsius.
2. Put pork sausages in your cooking basket, then cook within twenty-five mins, turning once till cooked.
3. Meanwhile, boil your pot with water and add potatoes. Cook within fifteen mins till soft. Strain, then add milk, butter, salt, plus pepper. Mash till smooth.
4. Slide open each slider bun, then spread some mashed potato on one side of your bun. Slice cooked sausages into halves, then put them on top.
5. Top with caramelized onions plus rocket leaves, then put top bun to close. Serve.

INGREDIENTS:

400 grams pork sausages
600 grams peeled & diced potatoes
200 millilitres milk
60 grams butter
Salt & pepper, as required
Eight slider buns
100 grams caramelized onions
50 grams rocket leaves

NUTRITIONAL VALUES (PER SERVING): CALORIES: 860, CARBS: 98G, FAT: 38G, PROTEIN: 38G

Lancashire
HOTPOT HAND PIES

🕐 **PREP:** *25 min*   🍲 **COOK:** *20 min*   🍴 **SERVES:** *6*

INGREDIENTS:

500 grams potatoes, thinly sliced
300 grams lamb, diced
200 grams onions, chopped
100 grams carrots, chopped
50 grams flour, all-purpose
300 millilitres beef or lamb stock
50 millilitres vegetable oil
One-litre hot water
Salt & pepper, as required
500 grams puff pastry

DIRECTIONS:

1. In your container, soak potatoes in hot water within ten mins. Strain, then put aside.
2. In your big pan, warm up oil on moderate temp. Add onions plus carrots, then cook within five mins till softened.
3. Mix in lamb, then cook within five mins till browned. Add flour, then mix well.
4. Pour beef stock, mixing it thickens. Flavour it using salt plus pepper. Remove, then cool it down.
5. Warm up your air fryer to 180 degrees Celsius.
6. Meanwhile, roll out your puff pastry to three millimetres thick. Slice out twelve circles.
7. Put six pastry circles on your flat surface, then spoon cooled lamb filling onto each circle's centre.
8. Top filled pastry circles using another puff pastry circle, then crimp their edges to seal them. Put pies into your cooking basket.
9. Cook within twenty mins till golden brown, flipping once. Remove, cool it down, then serve.

NUTRITIONAL VALUES (PER SERVING): CALORIES: 650, CARBS: 52G, FAT: 36G, PROTEIN: 27G

INGREDIENTS:

800 grams potatoes, washed & sliced into wedges
30 millilitres white vinegar
15 millilitres olive oil
Five grams sea salt
Two grams ground black pepper

Crispy Salt &
VINEGAR POTATO WEDGES

🕐 **PREP:** *10 min*   🍲 **COOK:** *25 min*   🍴 **SERVES:** *4*

DIRECTIONS:

1. In your big container, soak potato plus vinegar within ten mins. Strain, then pat dry.
2. Warm up your air fryer to 200 degrees Celsius.
3. In your separate container, mix oil, sea salt, plus pepper. Add potato wedges, then mix well.
4. Put potato wedges in your cooking basket. Cook within twenty-five mins, shaking your basket once. Serve.

NUTRITIONAL VALUES (PER SERVING): CALORIES: 210, CARBS: 38G, FAT: 4.5G, PROTEIN: 4G

Steak & Ale
PIE BITES

🕐 **PREP**: 20 min   🍲 **COOK**: 15 min   🍴 **SERVES**: 4

DIRECTIONS:

1. Put steak, onions, plus ale into your big pot. Cook within thirty mins on moderate temp till steak is tender.
2. In your separate pan, dissolve butter, then add flour, mixing till it a smooth paste form. Cook within two mins.
3. Slowly pour beef stock while mixing till it thickens.
4. Strain steak-onions, then mix with gravy mixture in your pan. Flavour it using salt plus pepper. Put aside.
5. Roll out puff pastry, then slice it into squares. Spoon cooled steak-ale filling onto half of each square, then fold it to seal.
6. Warm up your air fryer to 180 degrees Celsius. Put pie bites in your cooking basket, then cook within fifteen mins till golden brown.

INGREDIENTS:

500 grams diced steak
One litre ale
100 grams chopped onions
50 grams all-purpose flour
50 grams unsalted butter
200 millilitres beef stock
One-kilogram puff pastry, premade
Salt & pepper, as required

NUTRITIONAL VALUES (PER SERVING): CALORIES 892; CARBS 87G, FAT 60G, PROTEIN 35G

INGREDIENTS:

400 grams no bones & skin chicken breast, diced
300 grams puff pastry sheets
200 grams leeks, sliced
150 millilitres heavy cream
50 grams butter, unsalted
One egg, beaten
Salt & pepper, as required

Bangers &Creamy Leek & Chicken PUFF PASTRY PARCELS

🕐 **PREP**: 15 min   🍲 **COOK**: 25 min   🍴 **SERVES**: 4

DIRECTIONS:

1. Warm up your air fryer to 180 degrees Celsius.
2. In your pan on moderate temp, dissolve butter, then cook leeks within five mins. Add chicken, then cook till browned.
3. Mix in heavy cream, then cook within three mins. Flavour it using salt plus pepper. Remove, then cool it down.
4. Roll out puff pastry sheets on your lightly floured surface, then slice into eight squares.
5. Divide chicken-leek mixture among four squares. Brush each square edges using beaten egg.
6. Put an unlined puff pastry square on top of each filled square, then press to seal. Brush more beaten egg on top of each parcel.
7. Put parcels in your cooking basket. Cook within twenty mins till they are puffed up. Serve.

NUTRITIONAL VALUES (PER SERVING): CALORIES: 825, CARBS: 45G, FAT: 58G, PROTEIN: 36G

Plaice & Chips
WITH MUSHY PEAS

🕐 **PREP**: 15 min   🍲 **COOK**: 20 min   🍴 **SERVES**: 4

DIRECTIONS:

1. Warm up your air fryer to 180 degrees Celsius.
2. In your big container, mix potatoes, 15 millilitres oil plus salt.
3. Put chips in your cooking basket, then cook within twenty mins, shaking once, till crispy.
4. Meanwhile, put peas in your small saucepan with enough water. Let it boil, then cook within five mins. Strain, add milk, then mash till smooth. Flavour it using salt plus pepper.
5. Put plaice fillets in your cooking basket, then cook within seven to eight mins. Serve plaice fillets with chips plus mushy peas.

INGREDIENTS:

800 grams plaice fillets, washed & pat dried
800 grams potatoes, sliced into chips
300 grams frozen peas
50 millilitres milk
One-litre sunflower oil
Salt & pepper, as required

NUTRITIONAL VALUES (PER SERVING): CALORIES: 642, CARBS: 68G, FAT: 24G, PROTEIN: 45G

Ham & Pease
PUDDING SANDWICH

🕐 **PREP**: 15 min   🍲 **COOK**: 10 min   🍴 **SERVES**: 4

DIRECTIONS:

1. In your container, mix pease pudding, milk, salt, plus pepper till smooth. Put aside.
2. Warm up your air fryer to 180 degrees Celsius. Lay out your bread slices, then distribute ham on top.
3. Spread pease pudding mixture on each sandwich half. Put remaining bread slices on top to close.
4. Brush each sandwich using dissolved butter. Put sandwiches in your cooking basket. Cook within five mins per side till crispy. Serve.

INGREDIENTS:

400 grams pease pudding, pre-made
200 grams cooked ham, sliced
8 wholemeal bread slices
50 grams unsalted butter, melted
80 millilitres milk
Salt & pepper, as required

NUTRITIONAL VALUES (PER SERVING): CALORIES: 441, CARBS: 46G, FAT: 18G, PROTEIN: 24G

Spicy Lamb Kofta
WRAPS WITH YOGURT SAUCE

🕐 PREP: 20 min   📷 COOK: 20 min   🍴 SERVES: 4

DIRECTIONS:

1. In your big container, mix minced lamb, breadcrumbs, egg, garlic, cilantro, mint, cumin, coriander, cayenne pepper, salt, plus pepper.
2. Divide it into sixteen, then shape each into an elongated sausage shape.
3. Warm up your air fryer at 200 degrees Celsius.
4. Put koftas in your cooking basket, then cook within fifteen to twenty mins till cooked.
5. Meanwhile, mix yogurt, juice, dill, salt plus pepper. Put aside.
6. Put mixed salad leaves on each flatbread, then top with four koftas per wrap. Drizzle with the yogurt sauce, fold, then serve.

INGREDIENTS:

500 grams minced lamb
100 grams breadcrumbs
One whole egg
Five grams minced garlic clove
50 grams chopped cilantro
30 grams chopped fresh mint
Two grams ground cumin
Two grams ground coriander
One gram cayenne pepper
Salt & pepper, as required

For the yogurt sauce:
250 millilitres Greek yogurt
30 millilitres lemon juice
10 grams chopped dill
Salt & pepper, as required

For serving:
Four flatbreads, warmed
Mixed salad leaves

NUTRITIONAL VALUES (PER SERVING): CALORIES: 590, CARBS: 43G, FAT: 28G, PROTEIN: 42G

INGREDIENTS:

300 grams plain flour
150 grams cold butter, cubed, unsalted
50 millilitres ice water
Salt, as required
150 grams grated Cheddar cheese
200 grams cherry tomatoes, halved
100 grams vegetarian bacon, chopped
Three big eggs
250 millilitres milk
Salt & pepper, as required

Vegetarian Quiche Lorraine
WITH AIR FRIED CRUST

🕐 PREP: 20 min   📷 COOK: 30 min   🍴 SERVES: 4

DIRECTIONS:

1. In your big container, mix flour, salt, plus butter till crumbly.
2. Add ice water, then mix till a dough form. Wrap using your plastic wrap, then chill within one hour.
3. Roll out chilled dough on your floured surface. Press rolled dough into your air fryer-safe dish. Chill within fifteen mins.
4. Warm up your air fryer to 180 degrees Celsius. Line crust using baking paper, then weigh it down using a heavy object. Cook within ten mins.
5. Remove baking paper and heavy object, then cook within five mins till lightly golden.
6. Meanwhile, whisk eggs, milk, salt, plus pepper in your medium container. Scatter vegetarian bacon, tomatoes, plus half of cheese on top.
7. Pour it in your crust. Top it using rest of cheese. Cook within twenty mins till golden brown. Remove, cool it down, slice, then serve.

NUTRITIONAL VALUES (PER SERVING): CALORIES: 550, CARBS: 43G, FAT: 33G, PROTEIN: 23G

Chicken Tikka
MASALA PITA POCKETS

🕐 **PREP**: 20 min   📠 **COOK**: 8 min   🍴 **SERVES**: 4

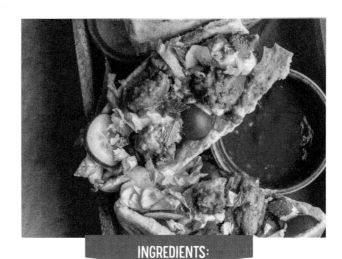

INGREDIENTS:

400 grams no bones & skin chicken breasts, cubes
200 millilitres yogurt
50 grams tikka masala paste
Four pita breads, toasted
100 grams mixed salad leaves
50 grams cucumber, thinly sliced
50 grams cherry tomatoes, halved
30 millilitres lemon juice
Salt & pepper, as required

DIRECTIONS:

1. In your container, mix chicken cubes, yogurt plus tikka masala paste. Marinate in your fridge within fifteen mins.
2. Warm up your air fryer to 200 degrees Celsius.
3. Put chicken pieces in your cooking basket, then cook within eight mins till cooked, shaking your basket one.
4. In your separate container, mix salad leaves, cucumber, tomatoes, juice, salt, plus pepper.
5. To assemble your pita pockets, slice a slit at one end of each pita bread, then stuff them with salad mixture.
6. Add cooked chicken tikka to each stuffed pita pocket. Serve.

NUTRITIONAL VALUES (PER SERVING): CALORIES: 415, CARBS: 48G, FAT: 6G, PROTEIN: 39G

INGREDIENTS:

Four ciabatta rolls
600 grams roast beef, pre-cooked & thinly sliced
150 millilitres horseradish sauce
100 grams mixed salad leaves
50 grams grated parmesan cheese
Olive oil for brushing
Salt & pepper, as required

Roast Beef
& Horseradish
CIABATTA ROLLS

🕐 **PREP**: 15 min   📠 **COOK**: 25 min   🍴 **SERVES**: 4

DIRECTIONS:

1. Warm up your air fryer to 180 degrees Celsius.
2. Slice ciabatta rolls in half lengthwise, then brush them using oil.
3. Put ciabatta rolls in your cooking basket. Cook within five mins till slightly crispy. Remove ciabatta rolls, then cool it down.
4. Spread horseradish sauce on bottom half of each roll. Divide roast beef slices among the four rolls, then put them on horseradish sauce.
5. Layer mixed salad leaves on roast beef, then sprinkle parmesan cheese. Top with rest of ciabatta halves, then flavour it using salt plus pepper.
6. Put assembled rolls back into your cooking basket, then cook within five to seven mins till heated.

NUTRITIONAL VALUES (PER SERVING): CALORIES: 510, CARBS: 34G, FAT: 20G, PROTEIN: 45G

Smoked Haddock
FISHCAKES WITH TARTARE DIP

🕐 **PREP**: 20 min   🍲 **COOK**: 20 min   🍴 **SERVES**: 4

DIRECTIONS:

1. In your big container, mix potatoes, flaked haddock, salt plus pepper. Shape into eight patties.
2. Prepare three containers containing flour, beaten eggs, and breadcrumbs; separately.
3. Coat each fishcake using flour, dip in beaten egg, then cover in breadcrumbs.
4. Warm up your air fryer at 200 degrees Celsius.
5. Put fishcakes into your cooking basket, then cook within twenty mins till crispy.
6. Meanwhile, mix yogurt, mayonnaise, capers, gherkins, and juice in your container to make tartare dip. Flavour it using salt plus pepper.
7. Serve smoked haddock fishcakes with tartare dip.

INGREDIENTS:

400 grams smoked haddock fillets, poached & flaked into small pieces
600 grams potatoes, peeled, diced, boiled, strained & mashed
100 grams breadcrumbs
2 large eggs, beaten
50 grams plain flour
Salt & pepper, as required

+For tartare dip:
200 grams Greek yogurt
50 millilitres mayonnaise
50 grams capers, chopped
50 grams gherkins, chopped
30 millilitres lemon juice
Salt & pepper, as required

NUTRITIONAL VALUES (PER SERVING): CALORIES: 510, CARBS: 50G, FAT: 20G, PROTEIN: 35G

Gammon Steak
SANDWICH WITH PINEAPPLE RELISH

🕐 **PREP**: 15 min   🍲 **COOK**: 20 min   🍴 **SERVES**: 2

DIRECTIONS:

1. Mix pineapple, onion, vinegar, brown sugar, salt, plus pepper in your small saucepan.
2. Cook on moderate temp within ten mins, mixing often till thickens. Put aside.
3. Warm up your air fryer to 180 degrees Celsius.
4. Rub gammon steaks using oil, then flavour it using salt plus pepper. Put steaks into your cooking basket, then cook within ten mins.
5. Flip them, then cook within ten mins till cooked. Spread pineapple relish onto one side of each bread slice.
6. Put cooked gammon steak on top, then add another toasted bread slice to close. Serve.

INGREDIENTS:

Two (250 grams each) gammon steaks
Four thick bread slices, toasted
30 millilitres olive oil
One pineapple, peeled, cored, & diced
100 grams red onion, finely chopped
60 millilitres apple cider vinegar
50 grams brown sugar
Salt & pepper, as required

NUTRITIONAL VALUES (PER SERVING): CALORIES: 960, CARBS: 75G, FAT: 38G, PROTEIN: 76G

Shepherd's Pie
EMPANADAS

🕐 **PREP**: 20 min   🍲 **COOK**: 15 min   🍴 **SERVES**: 6

DIRECTIONS:

1. In your big skillet, warm up oil on moderate temp. Add onions plus garlic, then cook till translucent.
2. Add minced lamb, breaking it up. Cook till browned. Add carrots, peas, Worcestershire, salt, plus pepper. Mix well.
3. Pour broth, then simmer within twenty mins till vegetables are tender.
4. Meanwhile, cook potatoes in boiling water till soft. Strain, mash, then put aside.
5. Warm up your air fryer to 180 degrees Celsius. Roll out empanada dough on your floured surface, then slice six circles.
6. Put mashed potatoes in each dough circle centre, then add lamb mixture on each. Fold it over, then press down to seal.
7. Put empanadas in your cooking basket, then cook within fifteen mins till golden brown, turning them once. Serve.

INGREDIENTS:

500 grams minced lamb
300 grams potatoes, cubed
150 grams each diced carrots & peas
200 grams onions, chopped
3 cloves garlic, minced
30 millilitres olive oil
One-litre beef broth
10 grams Worcestershire sauce
Salt & pepper, as required
500 grams empanada dough, prepared

NUTRITIONAL VALUES (PER SERVING): CALORIES: 675, CARBS: 49G, FAT: 35G, PROTEIN: 41G

INGREDIENTS:

Four English muffins, sliced in half
200g canned tuna, drained
160g sweetcorn, drained
120ml mayonnaise
100g grated cheddar cheese
Salt & pepper, as required

Tuna & Sweetcorn
MELTS ON TOASTED MUFFINS

🕐 **PREP**: 10 min   🍲 **COOK**: 6 min   🍴 **SERVES**: 4

DIRECTIONS:

1. Warm up your air fryer to 180 degrees Celsius.
2. Put English muffins halves in your cooking basket. Toast muffins within two mins till crisp.
3. In your medium container, mix tuna, sweetcorn, plus mayonnaise. Flavour it using salt plus pepper. Spoon it onto each muffin half. Sprinkle cheddar on top.
4. Put assembled muffin halves into your cooking basket. Cook within four mins till cheese is melted. Serve.

NUTRITIONAL VALUES (PER SERVING): CALORIES: 470, CARBS: 34G, FAT: 29G, PROTEIN: 21G

Braised Beef &
ONION FILLED YORKSHIRE PUDDINGS

🕐 PREP: 20 min   🍲 COOK: 40 min   🍴 SERVES: 6

DIRECTIONS:

1. In your pan on moderate temp, dissolve butter, then add onions plus salt. Cook till softened. Put aside.
2. Toss beef cubes in salt plus pepper. In your same pan, cook beef till browned on high temp.
3. Mix beef and onions in your pot with enough water. Cook on low temp within two hours till tender.
4. Meanwhile, mix flour, eggs, milk, plus salt till smooth. Let it rest within fifteen mins.
5. Warm up your air fryer to 180 degrees Celsius. Brush oil between six air fryer-safe ramekin dishes, then put them into your cooking basket to warm up.
6. Take warmed ramekins, then pour batter into each ramekin. Cook within twenty-five mins without opening.
7. Spoon braised beef-onion mixture into each Yorkshire pudding. Serve.

INGREDIENTS:

200 grams braising beef, cubed
150 grams onions, thinly sliced
125 grams all-purpose flour
Two big eggs
300 millilitres milk
30 millilitres sunflower oil
10 grams unsalted butter
Salt & pepper, as required

NUTRITIONAL VALUES (PER SERVING): CALORIES: 280, CARBS: 24G, FAT: 14G, PROTEIN: 16G

INGREDIENTS:

500 grams minced pork
One big apple, grated
100g breadcrumbs
75 grams small onion, chopped
Five grams sage, chopped
Salt & pepper, as required
Ten millilitres vegetable oil
250 millilitres apple cider
25 grams flour, all-purpose
240 millilitres chicken stock

Pork & Apple Sausage
PATTIES WITH CIDER GRAVY

🕐 PREP: 15 min   🍲 COOK: 25 min   🍴 SERVES: 4

DIRECTIONS:

1. In your container, mix minced pork, apple, breadcrumbs, onion, sage, salt, plus pepper. Form it into eight sausage patties.
2. Warm up your air fryer to 180 degrees Celsius. Brush sausage patties using oil.
3. Cook patties in your cooking basket within twenty mins till browned, flipping once.
4. Meanwhile, warm up rest of oil in your pan on moderate temp. Add flour, then cook within two mins while whisking till a smooth paste form.
5. Pour apple cider plus chicken stock while whisking. Simmer within five mins till it has thickened.
6. Serve cooked pork and apple sausage patties with cider gravy.

NUTRITIONAL VALUES (PER SERVING): CALORIES: 540, CARBS: 35G, FAT: 29G, PROTEIN: 28G

Beef Wellington Bites
WITH RED WINE REDUCTION

🕐 **PREP**: 15 min   🍲 **COOK**: 20 min   🍴 **SERVES**: 4

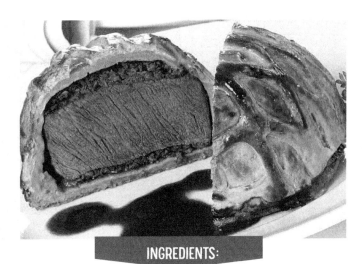

DIRECTIONS:

1. Warm up your air fryer to 190 degrees Celsius. Flavour beef tenderloin bites using salt plus pepper.
2. In your medium pan, warm up oil on moderate temp, then cook mushrooms and onions within five mins. Put aside.
3. Roll out your puff pastry, then slice into sixteen squares.
4. Put a prosciutto on each square of puff pastry, add mushroom and onion mixture, then add a piece of seasoned tenderloin on top.
5. Fold puff pastry on tenderloin, then press edges to seal. Brush each puff pastry bundle using beaten egg.
6. Put assembled beef bites in your cooking basket. Cook within fifteen to twenty mins till golden brown.
7. Meanwhile, mix red wine, broth, plus Worcestershire in your saucepan on moderate temp. Simmer till reduced, mixing often.
8. Remove, then whisk in butter. Serve beef wellington bites with red wine reduction.

INGREDIENTS:

500 grams beef tenderloin, cut into bite-sized pieces
Two grams salt
One-gram black pepper
200 grams puff pastry, thawed
100 grams chopped each mushrooms & onions
10 millilitres olive oil
50 grams prosciutto slices
One egg, beaten

Red Wine Reduction:
250 millilitres red wine
100 millilitres beef broth
10 millilitres Worcestershire sauce
20 grams unsalted butter

NUTRITIONAL VALUES (PER SERVING): CALORIES: 760, CARBS: 42G, FAT: 45G, PROTEIN: 41G

Chicken & Leek Pie
WITH PUFF PASTRY

🕐 **PREP**: 20 min   🍲 **COOK**: 30 min   🍴 **SERVES**: 4

DIRECTIONS:

1. Warm up your air fryer to 200 degrees Celsius.
2. In your big pan, dissolve butter on moderate temp, then add leeks. Cook within five to seven mins till softened.
3. Mix in flour, then cook within one min, mixing. Pour chicken stock plus milk while mixing. Simmer within five mins till thickened.
4. Add cubed chicken, salt plus pepper, then cook within five mins till cooked.
5. Roll out puff pastry on your floured surface. Spoon chicken-leek mixture into your baking dish.
6. Lay puff pastry on filling, pressing edges to seal. Slice a few slits on top of your pastry.
7. Put baking dish in your cooking basket, then cook within twenty to twenty-five mins till golden brown.

INGREDIENTS:

500 grams no bones & skin chicken breasts, cubed
200 grams leeks, chopped & washed
300 grams puff pastry, ready-made
30 grams each butter & plain flour
350 millilitres chicken stock
150 millilitres milk
Salt & pepper, as required

NUTRITIONAL VALUES (PER SERVING): CALORIES: 436, CARBS: 36G, FAT: 27G, PROTEIN: 22G

Lamb Shank
SHEPHERD'S PIE

🕐 **PREP**: 30 min   🍲 **COOK**: 60 min   🍴 **SERVES**: 4

DIRECTIONS:

1. Warm up your air fryer to 180 degrees Celsius.
2. Put lamb shanks in your cooking basket, then cook within forty-five mins, turning once.
3. Meanwhile, boil potatoes in your big pot with water till fork tender.
4. Strain potatoes, then mash with butter plus milk till smooth. Flavour it using salt plus pepper. Put aside.
5. In your big pan, cook carrots plus onions on medium heat till soft. Add garlic, then cook within one min.
6. Remove cooked lamb, then shred it. Add it to your pan with vegetables along with peas, beef stock, plus Worcestershire.
7. Simmer within fifteen mins till liquid has reduced by half.
8. Transfer it into your oven-safe dish, then spread mashed potatoes on top.
9. Put dish into your cooking basket, then cook within fifteen mins till potato topping is golden brown.

INGREDIENTS:

800 grams lamb shanks
One-kilogram potatoes, peeled & chopped
50 grams butter
100 millilitres milk
200 grams carrots, chopped
200 grams onions, chopped
Two cloves garlic, minced
200 grams frozen peas
One litre beef stock
30 millilitres Worcester-shire sauce
Salt & pepper, as required

NUTRITIONAL VALUES (PER SERVING): CALORIES: 750, CARBS: 65G, FAT: 35G, PROTEIN: 45G

INGREDIENTS:

800 grams pork tenderloin, sliced into two-cm-thick
Three grams salt
One-gram black pepper, ground
15 millilitres olive oil
400 grams Granny Smith apples, sliced
240 millilitres dry cider
80 millilitres chicken stock
120 millilitres cream

Pork Medallions
WITH APPLE & CIDER SAUCE

🕐 **PREP**: 10 min   🍲 **COOK**: 20 min   🍴 **SERVES**: 4

DIRECTIONS:

1. Warm up your air fryer to 200 degrees Celsius. Flavour pork medallions using salt plus black pepper.
2. Brush oil on pork medallions.
3. Transfer it in your cooking basket, then cook within ten mins, flipping once. Remove pork, then cool it down.
4. In your pan on moderate temp, add apples, cider, plus chicken stock. Cook within five mins.
5. Add cream, then simmer within five mins till slightly thickened. Serve pork medallions with apple & cider sauce on top.

NUTRITIONAL VALUES (PER SERVING): CALORIES: 570, CARBS: 26G, FAT: 31G, PROTEIN: 45G

Crispy Cod & Chips
WITH PEA PURÉE

🕐 **PREP**: 15 min   🍲 **COOK**: 20 min   🍴 **SERVES**: 4

DIRECTIONS:

1. Warm up your air fryer to 200 degrees Celsius.
2. In your shallow container, mix flour, salt plus pepper. In another container, whisk two eggs. Put breadcrumbs in your third container.
3. Coat each cod fillet in flour mixture, dip into eggs, then roll in breadcrumbs. Spray your coated fish & chips using oil spray.
4. Put chips in your cooking basket, then cook within ten mins.
5. Add breaded cod fillets & chips to your cooking basket, then cook within ten mins till golden brown.
6. Put cooked peas, milk plus butter in your saucepan. Blend using your hand blender till smooth.
7. Flavour pea purée using salt plus pepper. Serve.

INGREDIENTS:

800 grams cod fillets
800 grams potatoes, cut into chips
100 grams each plain flour & breadcrumbs
Two eggs
Salt & pepper, as required
Oil spray
500 grams frozen peas, cooked & strained
50 millilitres milk
50 grams unsalted butter

NUTRITIONAL VALUES (PER SERVING): CALORIES: 718, CARBS: 75G, FAT: 23G, PROTEIN: 51G

Creamy Chicken &
MUSHROOM FRICASSEE

🕐 **PREP**: 15 min   🍲 **COOK**: 20 min   🍴 **SERVES**: 4

DIRECTIONS:

1. In your big container, toss chicken, mushrooms, oil, salt, plus pepper.
2. Warm up your air fryer to 190 degrees Celsius.
3. Put chicken and mushrooms in your cooking basket, then cook within ten mins. Put aside.
4. In your separate pan on moderate temp, cook onion plus garlic within five mins till tender.
5. Add flour, then cook within one min, mixing. Slowly whisk in broth plus heavy cream. Mix within three mins till thickened.
6. Mix cooked chicken and mushrooms with creamy sauce. Serve.

INGREDIENTS:

800 grams no bones & skin chicken breast, sliced into bite-sized pieces
200 grams mushrooms, sliced
30 millilitres olive oil
150 grams diced onion
10 grams garlic, minced
50 grams flour, all-purpose
250 millilitres chicken broth
100 millilitres heavy cream
Salt & pepper, as required

NUTRITIONAL VALUES (PER SERVING): CALORIES: 498, CARBS: 16G, FAT: 22G, PROTEIN: 58G

Pulled Pork Sliders
WITH COLESLAW

🕐 **PREP**: 30 min   ▦ **COOK**: 1 Hour   🍴 **SERVES**: 4

DIRECTIONS:

1. Warm up your air fryer to 180 degrees Celsius. Flavour pork shoulder using salt, plus pepper, then coat it with half barbecue sauce.
2. Put pork shoulder in your cooking basket, then cook within one hour, turning once.
3. In your big container, mix cabbage, carrots, mayonnaise, vinegar, salt plus pepper. Remove, then let it rest within ten mins.
4. Shred pork using two forks, then mix it with rest of barbecue sauce. Put some pulled pork on each slider bun, then top it with coleslaw. Serve.

INGREDIENTS:

One-kilogram pork shoulder
400 grams barbecue sauce
200 grams slider buns
200 grams shredded cabbage
100 grams grated carrots
150 millilitres mayonnaise
50 millilitres apple cider vinegar
Salt & pepper, as required

NUTRITIONAL VALUES (PER SERVING): CALORIES: 850, CARBS: 85G, FAT: 40G, PROTEIN: 40G

Traditional Fisherman's
Pie WITH AIR FRIED TOPPING

🕐 **PREP**: 20 min   ▦ **COOK**: 40 min   🍴 **SERVES**: 4

DIRECTIONS:

1. Warm up your air fryer to 180 degrees Celsius.
2. In your big pot, add white fish and smoked fish fillets. Add milk, then simmer within ten mins on low temp.
3. Meanwhile, cook potatoes in your separate pot filled with boiling water within twenty mins. Starin, then mash potatoes with salt plus pepper.
4. Remove fish, then flake into big pieces in your ovenproof dish. Reserve the milk.
5. In your saucepan, dissolve butter on moderate temp. Slowly add flour while mixing till you have a smooth paste.
6. Slowly whisk in reserved milk, then cook till it thickens. Mix in parsley into your sauce, then flavour it using salt plus pepper.
7. Pour sauce on flaked fish pieces in your ovenproof dish. Top with mashed potatoes. Sprinkle cheddar on top. Cook within twenty mins till crispy. Serve.

INGREDIENTS:

400 grams white fish fillet
200 grams smoked fish fillet
One-litre milk
50 grams butter
50 grams plain flour
One-kilogram potatoes, peeled & chopped
10 grams parsley, chopped
Salt & black pepper, as required
100 grams cheddar cheese, grated

NUTRITIONAL VALUES (PER SERVING): CALORIES: 565, CARBS: 105G, FAT: 18G, PROTEIN: 39G

Braised Beef Ribs
WITH STICKY GLAZE

🕐 **PREP:** 15 min　　📟 **COOK:** 45 min　　🍴 **SERVES:** 4

DIRECTIONS:

1. Warm up your air fryer to 180 degrees Celsius. Flavour beef ribs using salt and pepper.
2. In your big skillet, warm up oil on moderate-high temp. Add beef ribs, then sear within two mins per side. Transfer to your plate, then put aside.
3. In your same skillet, add onions, then cook within two to three mins till softened. Add garlic, then cook within one min.
4. Add broth, dark brown sugar, vinegar, plus Worcestershire. Let it boil, then simmer within five mins. Add beef ribs, then mix well.
5. Transfer it into your air-fryer safe baking dish. Put baking dish in your cooking basket, then cook within forty-five mins till ribs are tender.
6. Remove, cool it down, then serve.

INGREDIENTS:

One-kilogram beef short ribs
One gram salt
One-gram black pepper, ground
30 millilitres olive oil
100 grams diced onion
Two grams minced garlic
500 millilitres beef broth
60 grams dark brown sugar
60 millilitres apple cider vinegar
30 millilitres Worcestershire sauce

NUTRITIONAL VALUES (PER SERVING): CALORIES: 682, CARBS: 17G, FAT: 44G, PROTEIN: 52G

Chicken Kiev
WITH GARLIC BUTTER

🕐 **PREP:** 20 min　　📟 **COOK:** 25 min　　🍴 **SERVES:** 4

DIRECTIONS:

1. In your small container, mix butter, garlic, juice, salt, plus pepper.
2. Slit a pocket in each chicken breast. Fill each pocket with garlic butter, then press edges to seal.
3. Put flour on your flat plate, beat eggs in your shallow container, put breadcrumbs on another plate.
4. Coat each stuffed chicken breast in flour, dip it into eggs, then cover using breadcrumbs.
5. Warm up your air fryer to 180 degrees Celsius. Put breaded chicken breasts in your cooking basket.
6. Cook within twenty-five mins till golden brown. Serve.

INGREDIENTS:

Four no bones & skin chicken breasts
200 grams butter, softened, unsalted
20 grams garlic cloves, minced
15 millilitres lemon juice
Salt & black pepper, as required
200 grams flour, all-purpose
Three big eggs, beaten
200 grams breadcrumbs

NUTRITIONAL VALUES (PER SERVING): CALORIES: 740, CARBS: 53G, FAT: 37G, PROTEIN: 52G

Lamb Moussaka
WITH AIR FRIED AUBERGINE

🕐 **PREP**: 30 min   📦 **COOK**: 50 min   🍴 **SERVES**: 6

DIRECTIONS:

1. Warm up your air fryer to 190 degrees Celsius.
2. Brush aubergine slices using oil, then flavour it using salt plus pepper.
3. Put them in your cooking basket, then cook within ten mins, turning them once. Put aside.
4. In your big pan, warm up 30 millilitres oil on moderate temp. Put onions plus garlic, then cook within five mins.
5. Add minced lamb, then cook within eight mins till browned. Mix in tomatoes, oregano, cinnamon, salt, plus pepper. Adjust to a simmer within fifteen mins.
6. In your small saucepan, warm up milk on low temp.
7. Layer half of air fried aubergine slices, add lamb mixture, then another layer of aubergine slices in your ovenproof dish.
8. Pour warmed milk, then sprinkle cheddar on top.
9. Warm up your oven to 180 degrees Celsius, then bake within twenty-five mins till golden. Remove, cool it down, then serve.

INGREDIENTS:

500 grams minced lamb
700 grams aubergines, sliced
400 grams chopped tomatoes
250 millilitres milk
150 grams grated cheddar cheese
100 grams onions, chopped
50 millilitres olive oil
Five grams clove garlic, minced
Two grams oregano, dried
One gram cinnamon, ground
Salt & pepper, as required

NUTRITIONAL VALUES (PER SERVING): CALORIES: 473, CARBS: 19.2G, FAT: 34.1G, PROTEIN: 23.4G

INGREDIENTS:

800 grams pork shoulder, cut into 3cm cubes
200 millilitres dry cider
One big onion, chopped
Two cloves garlic, minced
Two carrots, peeled & sliced
150 grams mushrooms, sliced
400 grams chopped tomatoes
250 grams sliced potatoes
30 grams flat-leaf parsley, chopped
50 grams butter, melted
Salt & pepper, as required

Pork & Cider Casserole
WITH PARSLEY CRUST

🕐 **PREP**: 20 min   📦 **COOK**: 45 min   🍴 **SERVES**: 4

DIRECTIONS:

1. Warm up your air fryer to 180 degrees Celsius.
2. In your big container, mix pork cubes using salt plus pepper.
3. Put pork in your cooking basket, then cook within twenty mins till browned, mixing often.
4. In your separate pan on moderate temp, add butter, then cook onions plus garlic within five mins or till softened.
5. Add carrots and mushrooms, then cook within five mins. Mix in canned tomatoes and cider, then simmer. Add cooked pork, then mix well.
6. Transfer casserole mixture to your baking dish. Layer potatoes on top, then brush using butter. Sprinkle parsley on top.
7. Cook within twenty-five mins till potatoes are crispy.

NUTRITIONAL VALUES (PER SERVING): CALORIES: 600, CARBS: 35G, FAT: 32G, PROTEIN: 40G

Haddock &
LEEK GRATIN

🕐 **PREP**: 15 min   🍲 **COOK**: 20 min   🍴 **SERVES**: 4

DIRECTIONS:

1. Warm up your air fryer to 180 degrees Celsius.
2. In your pan, warm up oil on moderate temp, then cook leeks within four mins.
3. Mix in double cream then cook within two mins, then flavour it using salt plus pepper.
4. Put haddock fillets in your cooking basket. Spoon creamy leek mixture on top.
5. In your small container, mix cheddar and breadcrumbs. Sprinkle this mixture on haddock fillets.
6. Cook within twenty mins till golden brown on top. Serve.

INGREDIENTS:

800 grams haddock fillets
500 grams leeks, cleaned & sliced
200 millilitres double cream
100 grams cheddar cheese, grated
50 grams breadcrumbs
30 millilitres olive oil
Salt & pepper, as required

NUTRITIONAL VALUES (PER SERVING): CALORIES: 628, CARBS: 24G, FAT: 38G, PROTEIN: 47G

Beef Stroganoff
WITH AIR FRIED RICE

🕐 **PREP**: 15 min   🍲 **COOK**: 30 min   🍴 **SERVES**: 4

DIRECTIONS:

1. Warm up your air fryer to 200 degrees Celsius.
2. In your big container, mix cooked basmati rice with 25 millilitres oil.
3. Transfer rice to your cooking basket, then cook within ten mins, mixing once.
4. In your big skillet, warm up remaining oil on moderate-high temp. Add beef, then flavour it using salt plus pepper. Cook till browned, remove, then put aside.
5. In your same skillet, add onion plus garlic, then cook till softened. Add mushrooms, then cook within five mins.
6. Mix in tomato paste, then cook within two mins, then add broth. Let it boil, then simmer within five mins.
7. Add sour cream while mixing. Add browned beef, then cook within three mins. Serve beef stroganoff on air fried rice.

INGREDIENTS:

500 grams beef sirloin, thin strips
400 grams cooked basmati rice
200 grams white button mushrooms, sliced
150 grams medium onion, chopped
10 grams cloves garlic, minced
250 millilitres beef broth
150 millilitres sour cream
50 millilitres olive oil, divided
30 grams tomato paste
Salt & pepper, as required

NUTRITIONAL VALUES (PER SERVING): CALORIES: 715, CARBS: 58G, FAT: 32G, PROTEIN: 47G

Minted Lamb Chops
WITH ROSEMARY POTATOES

🕐 **PREP:** *15 min*   🍱 **COOK:** *20 min*   🍴 **SERVES:** *4*

DIRECTIONS:

1. In your small container, mix mint, garlic, plus 25 millilitres oil. Put aside.
2. Flavour lamb chops using salt plus black pepper. Coat each lamb chop using mint mixture.
3. In another container, toss baby potatoes with remaining oil, rosemary, salt, plus pepper.
4. Warm up your air fryer to 180 degrees Celsius. Put lamb chops in your cooking basket. Add seasoned potatoes around lamb chops.
5. Cook within twenty mins, turning lamb chops and shaking potatoes once. Serve.

INGREDIENTS:

Eight lamb chops (800 grams), pat dried
20 grams mint leaves, chopped
10 grams garlic cloves, minced
50 millilitres olive oil
One-kilogram baby potatoes, halved
Ten grams rosemary, chopped
Salt & black pepper, as required

NUTRITIONAL VALUES (PER SERVING): CALORIES: 780, CARBS: 55G, FAT: 41G, PROTEIN: 52G

INGREDIENTS:

400 grams pork tenderloin, sliced into four
100 grams plain flour
Two eggs, beaten
200 grams breadcrumbs
Zest of one lemon
20 grams parsley, chopped
Salt & pepper, as required
Ten millilitres vegetable oil
One lemon, cut into wedges

Pork Schnitzel
WITH LEMON & PARSLEY

🕐 **PREP:** *15 min*   🍱 **COOK:** *10 min*   🍴 **SERVES:** *4*

DIRECTIONS:

1. Put cling film on each pork slice, then pound them.
2. Prepare three shallow containers, mix flour, salt plus pepper in first. Beat two eggs in second. Mix breadcrumbs, zest, plus parsley in third container.
3. Coat each pork slice in seasoned flour, dip in beaten egg, then press into breadcrumb mixture.
4. Warm up your air fryer to 180 degrees Celsius. Brush each breaded pork slice using oil. Put them in your cooking basket.
5. Cook within five mins per side till crispy. Transfer cooked pork schnitzels onto your plate, then serve with lemon wedges.

NUTRITIONAL VALUES (PER SERVING): CALORIES: 525, CARBS: 53G, FAT: 17G, PROTEIN: 42G

Salmon en Croûte
WITH DILL SAUCE

🕐 **PREP**: 20 min   🍲 **COOK**: 20 min   🍴 **SERVES**: 4

DIRECTIONS:

1. Warm up your air fryer to 200 degrees Celsius. Flavour salmon fillet using salt plus pepper.
2. Roll out puff pastry into a thin rectangle, then put salmon in centre. Seal puff pastry edges, then brush using beaten egg.
3. Cook wrapped salmon in your cooking basket within twenty mins till golden brown.
4. In your small saucepan, mix crème fraîche, milk, dill, zest, juice, plus salt. Warm up while mixing.
5. Remove cooked Salmon en Croûte, cool it down, then slice it. Serve Salmon en Croûte slices with warm dill sauce on top.

INGREDIENTS:

400 grams skinless salmon fillet
200 grams puff pastry
Salt & pepper, as required
One egg, beaten
200 millilitres crème fraîche
50 millilitres whole milk
20 grams dill, finely chopped
Zest of one lemon
Juice of half a lemon

NUTRITIONAL VALUES (PER SERVING): CALORIES: 615, CARBS: 40G, FAT: 41G, PROTEIN: 25G

Spaghetti Bolognese
BAKE WITH CHEESY CRUST

🕐 **PREP**: 20 min   **COOK**: 30 min   **SERVES**: 4

DIRECTIONS:

1. Boil your big pot with salted water, then cook spaghetti till tender. Strain, then put aside.
2. In your big non-stick pan, warm up oil on moderate temp. Add onion plus garlic, then cook till softened.
3. Add minced beef, breaking it up, then cook till browned. Mix in tomato passata and tomatoes. Flavour it using salt plus pepper.
4. Warm up your air fryer to 180 degrees Celsius. In your big baking dish, mix spaghetti plus Bolognese sauce.
5. Sprinkle cheddar plus parmesan cheese on top. Put baking dish in your cooking basket, then cook within fifteen mins till cheese is melted.

INGREDIENTS:

400 grams spaghetti
500 grams minced beef
300 grams tomato passata
200 grams cherry tomatoes, halved
One small onion, chopped
Two cloves garlic, minced
30 millilitres olive oil
Salt & pepper, as required
100 grams cheddar cheese, grated
50 grams parmesan cheese, grated

NUTRITIONAL VALUES (PER SERVING): CALORIES: 701, CARBS: 64G, FAT: 31G, PROTEIN: 47G

Stuffed Chicken Breasts
WITH SUNDRIED TOMATOES

🕐 **PREP**: 15 min   🍲 **COOK**: 20 min   🍴 **SERVES**: 4

DIRECTIONS:

1. Warm up your air fryer to 180 degrees Celsius.
2. In your small container, mix tomatoes, basil, mozzarella, plus Parmesan cheese. Flavour it using salt plus pepper.
3. Slice a pocket in each chicken breast. Stuff each with tomato-basil mixture.
4. In your shallow container, lightly whisk eggs. Spread breadcrumbs in another shallow container.
5. Dip each stuffed chicken breast into eggs, then coat using breadcrumbs.
6. Put coated chicken breasts into your oiled cooking basket. Cook within twenty mins till cooked, flipping once.

INGREDIENTS:

Four no bones & skin chicken breasts
100 grams sundried tomatoes, chopped
50 grams basil leaves, chopped
200 grams mozzarella cheese, grated
40 grams grated Parmesan cheese
Salt & pepper, as required
Two eggs
100 grams breadcrumbs
50 millilitres olive oil

NUTRITIONAL VALUES (PER SERVING): CALORIES: 588, CARBS: 21G, FAT: 28G, PROTEIN: 64G

INGREDIENTS:

500 grams diced lamb
200 grams chopped mixed vegetables
150 grams onion, chopped
Three garlic cloves, minced
20 grams curry paste
400 millilitres diced tomatoes, canned
200 millilitres coconut milk
Ten grams vegetable oil
Salt & pepper, as required

For Poppadoms:
Eight store-bought poppadoms
Oil spray

Lamb & Vegetable
CURRY WITH POPPADOMS

🕐 **PREP**: 20 min   🍲 **COOK**: 30 min   🍴 **SERVES**: 4

DIRECTIONS:

1. Warm up your air fryer to 200 degrees Celsius.
2. In your big container, mix diced lamb, onions, garlic, plus curry paste. Put aside within ten mins.
3. Toss marinated lamb mixture with mixed vegetables. Coat your cooking basket using oil.
4. Transfer lamb and vegetable mixture to your cooking basket, then cook within twenty mins, mixing once.
5. Add diced tomatoes plus coconut milk. Cook within ten mins. Flavour it using salt plus pepper.
6. Meanwhile, spray each poppadom using oil spray. Put them in your cooking basket, then cook within two mins, flipping once.
7. Serve lamb and vegetable curry with crisp poppadoms.

NUTRITIONAL VALUES (PER SERVING): CALORIES: 445, CARBS: 22G, FAT: 29G, PROTEIN: 25G

Pork Loin Steaks
WITH MUSTARD & CREAM SAUCE

🕐 **PREP**: 15 min   🍲 **COOK**: 20 min   🍴 **SERVES**: 4

DIRECTIONS:

1. Warm up your air fryer to 190 degrees Celsius. Flavour pork loin steaks using salt plus pepper. Brush steaks using oil.
2. Put steaks into your cooking basket. Cook steaks within ten mins, flip them, then cook within ten mins till cooked,
3. In your small saucepan, warm up heavy cream on moderate-low temp till just warmed. Whisk in mustard till blended.
4. Arrange green beans on each plate, top with pork loin steak, then drizzle using mustard cream sauce.

INGREDIENTS:

Four pork loin steaks
150 millilitres heavy cream
30 grams Dijon mustard
15 millilitres olive oil
Salt & pepper, as required
150 grams green beans, trimmed, halved & steamed
75 millilitres water

NUTRITIONAL VALUES (PER SERVING): CALORIES: 421, CARBS: 4G, FAT: 31G, PROTEIN: 32G

INGREDIENTS:

Four (200 grams each) whole sea bass fillets
400 grams cherry tomatoes
200 grams courgette, thin rounds
150 grams red bell pepper, chopped
100 grams Kalamata olives, halved
50 millilitres olive oil
50 millilitres lemon juice
Salt & pepper, as required

Sea Bass
WITH MEDITERRANEAN VEGETABLES

🕐 **PREP**: 15 min   🍲 **COOK**: 20 min   🍴 **SERVES**: 4

DIRECTIONS:

1. In your big container, mix cherry tomatoes, courgette, bell pepper, plus olives. Drizzle with half of oil, Flavour it using salt plus pepper. Toss gently.
2. Warm up your air fryer to 180 degrees Celsius.
3. Flavour sea bass fillets using salt plus pepper. Put a layer of prepared vegetables in your cooking basket, then put fillets on top. Cook within twelve to fifteen mins.
4. Meanwhile, mix rest of oil plus juice in your small container. Remove fish fillets and vegetables. Drizzle each with some dressing. Serve.

NUTRITIONAL VALUES (PER SERVING): CALORIES: 445, CARBS: 12G, FAT: 29G, PROTEIN: 35G

Lamb Tagine
WITH APRICOTS & ALMONDS

🕐 **PREP**: 20 min   🍲 **COOK**: 30 min   🍴 **SERVES**: 4

DIRECTIONS:

1. In your container, mix lamb cubes, cumin, cinnamon, salt, plus black pepper. Put aside within ten mins.
2. Warm up your air fryer to 180 degrees Celsius.
3. Put marinated lamb inside your cooking basket. Cook within fifteen mins till browned.
4. Meanwhile, in your big saucepan on moderate temp, add onions plus garlic. Cook till softened.
5. Add cooked lamb, vegetable stock, tomatoes, butternut squash, apricots, plus almonds.
6. Let it boil, then adjust to low temp. Simmer within fifteen mins till sauce thickens. Serve.

INGREDIENTS:

500 grams lamb, cubed
100 grams dried apricots, chopped
50 grams almonds, toasted & chopped
200 grams onions, chopped
Two cloves garlic, minced
300 millilitres vegetable stock
400 grams chopped tomatoes, canned
200 grams butternut squash, cubed
Ten grams cumin, ground
Seven grams cinnamon, ground
Salt & black pepper, as required

NUTRITIONAL VALUES (PER SERVING): CALORIES: 510, CARBS: 38G, FAT: 22G, PROTEIN: 38G

INGREDIENTS:

800 grams pork belly slices
30 millilitres olive oil
Ten grams fennel seeds
Five grams salt
Two grams black pepper
200 grams baby potatoes, halved
150 grams cherry tomatoes
50 millilitres balsamic vinegar

Pork Belly Slices
WITH FENNEL SEEDS

🕐 **PREP**: 10 min   🍲 **COOK**: 20 min   🍴 **SERVES**: 4

DIRECTIONS:

1. Warm up your air fryer to 180 degrees Celsius.
2. In your container, mix pork belly slices, oil, fennel seeds, salt, plus pepper.
3. Put seasoned pork belly slices in your cooking basket. Cook within ten mins per side till crispy. Remove pork belly slices, then cool it down.
4. Meanwhile, toss baby potatoes plus cherry tomatoes in remaining oil. Flavour it using salt plus pepper.
5. Place the seasoned potatoes and tomatoes in your cooking basket then cook within eight mins, shaking halfway through cooking.
6. Drizzle balsamic vinegar on cooked potatoes plus tomatoes. Serve pork belly slices with balsamic roasted potatoes and tomatoes.

NUTRITIONAL VALUES (PER SERVING): CALORIES: 750, CARBS: 25G, FAT: 60G, PROTEIN: 35G

Trout with Almonds & BROWN BUTTER

🕐 **PREP**: *15 min*   📋 **COOK**: *10 min*   🍴 **SERVES**: *2*

DIRECTIONS:

1. Warm up your air fryer to 180 degrees Celsius.
2. Flavour inside cavities of each trout using salt plus pepper.
3. In your shallow plate, mix flour, salt plus pepper. Coat trouts in seasoned flour.
4. Put seasoned trouts in your cooking basket. Cook within ten mins till cooked.
5. Meanwhile, warm up butter in your small saucepan on moderate-high temp. Add sliced almonds then cook within two mins till golden brown. Remove butter, then mix in lemon juice.
6. Remove cooked trouts onto serving plates. Spoon almond and brown butter sauce on each trout. Serve.

INGREDIENTS:

Two whole trouts (500 grams each), cleaned, gutted & pat dried
30 grams flour, all-purpose
Salt & pepper, as required
60 grams unsalted butter
60 grams almonds, sliced
15 millilitres lemon juice

NUTRITIONAL VALUES (PER SERVING): CALORIES: 922, CARBS: 13G, FAT: 65G, PROTEIN: 74G

Beef & Mushroom STIR-FRY WITH EGG NOODLES

🕐 **PREP**: *15 min*   📋 **COOK**: *20 min*   🍴 **SERVES**: *4*

DIRECTIONS:

1. Mix soy sauce, oyster sauce, plus cornstarch in your big container. Add beef strips, then marinate within ten mins.
2. Warm up your air fryer to 200 degrees Celsius.
3. Meanwhile, cook egg noodles till tender, strain, then put aside.
4. Toss beef strips plus mushrooms in your cooking basket, then cook within eight mins, shaking once.
5. In your big pan, warm up fifteen millilitres oil on moderate temp. Put onion plus garlic, then cook till fragrant.
6. Add bell pepper, then cook within three mins. Transfer beef strips-mushrooms mixture to your pan, mixing well. Add cooked egg noodles, then toss well.

INGREDIENTS:

500 grams beef strips
300 grams egg noodles
200 grams mushrooms, sliced
100 millilitres soy sauce
50 millilitres oyster sauce
One litre vegetable oil
30 grams cornstarch
200 grams bell pepper, sliced
100 grams onion, chopped
Two minced cloves garlic

NUTRITIONAL VALUES (PER SERVING): CALORIES: 600, CARBS: 68G, FAT: 20G, PROTEIN: 38G

Rosemary Chicken
THIGHS WITH ROASTED VEGETABLES

🕐 **PREP**: 15 min   ▣ **COOK**: 25 min   🍴 **SERVES**: 4

DIRECTIONS:

1. In your big container, mix oil, rosemary, salt, plus pepper. Add chicken thighs, then mix again. Marinate within fifteen mins.
2. Warm up your air fryer to 180 degrees Celsius. Put marinated chicken thighs in your cooking basket, then cook within ten mins.
3. In another container, mix baby potatoes, vegetables, plus vinegar. Add it to your cooking basket. Cook within fifteen mins. Serve.

INGREDIENTS:

800 grams bone-in & skin-on chicken thighs
30 millilitres olive oil
Two grams chopped rosemary
Two grams salt
One-gram black pepper
400 grams baby potatoes, halved
300 grams mixed vegetables, chopped
50 millilitres balsamic vinegar

NUTRITIONAL VALUES (PER SERVING): CALORIES: 590, CARBS: 39G, FAT: 30G, PROTEIN: 42G

Lamb & Mint Meatballs
WITH TOMATO SAUCE

🕐 **PREP**: 15 min   ▣ **COOK**: 20 min   🍴 **SERVES**: 4

DIRECTIONS:

1. In your big container, mix lamb mince, breadcrumbs, egg, mint, garlic, salt, plus pepper. Shape it into small meatballs.
2. Warm up your air fryer to 200 degrees Celsius. Put meatballs into your cooking basket, then cook within ten mins.
3. In your saucepan on moderate temp, mix passata, water, plus oregano. Cook within five mins till slightly thickened.
4. Add cooked meatballs, then cook within three mins. Serve.

INGREDIENTS:

500 grams lamb mince
50 grams breadcrumbs
One big beaten egg
Five grams chopped mint leaves
One clove minced garlic
Salt & pepper, as required
250 millilitres passata
100 millilitres water
Five grams chopped oregano

NUTRITIONAL VALUES (PER SERVING): CALORIES: 368, CARBS: 17G, FAT: 21G, PROTEIN: 30G

Honey & Mustard
GLAZED PORK RIBS

🕐 **PREP:** 15 min   🍲 **COOK:** 25 min   🍴 **SERVES:** 4

DIRECTIONS:

1. In your small container, mix honey, mustard, soy sauce, Worcestershire, plus vinegar. Flavour pork ribs using salt plus pepper.
2. Pour honey-mustard mixture on seasoned ribs. Marinate within one hour in your refrigerator.
3. Warm up your air fryer to 180 degrees Celsius. Put marinated ribs in your cooking basket. Cook within twenty-five mins, flipping once. Serve.

INGREDIENTS:

One kilogram pork ribs
60 millilitres each honey & whole grain mustard
30 millilitres soy sauce
15 millilitres each Worcestershire sauce & apple cider vinegar
One gram each salt & black pepper

NUTRITIONAL VALUES (PER SERVING): CALORIES: 750, CARBS: 21G, FAT: 53G, PROTEIN: 50G

INGREDIENTS:

400 grams smoked, skinned & flaked mackerel fillets
150 grams cream cheese, full-fat
10 millilitres lemon juice
15 millilitres horseradish sauce
Salt & black pepper, as required
Five grams chopped each parsley & dill
100 grams brioche slices

Smoked Mackerel Pâté
WITH TOASTED BRIOCHE

🕐 **PREP:** 15 min   🍲 **COOK:** 5 min   🍴 **SERVES:** 4

DIRECTIONS:

1. Put smoked mackerel, cream cheese, juice, plus horseradish sauce in your food processor. Flavour it using salt plus pepper, then blend till smooth.
2. Transfer it to your container, then fold in parsley plus dill. Warm up your air fryer to 180 degrees Celsius.
3. Put brioche slices in your cooking basket. Cook within four to five mins till crispy, turning once. Remove toasted brioche slices, then cool it down.
4. Spread pâté on each toasted brioche slice. Serve.

NUTRITIONAL VALUES (PER SERVING): CALORIES: 488, CARBS: 26G, FAT: 32G, PROTEIN: 29G

Spinach & Ricotta
STUFFED PORTOBELLO MUSHROOMS

🕐 **PREP**: 15 min   🍲 **COOK**: 15 min   🍴 **SERVES**: 4

DIRECTIONS:

1. Warm up your air fryer to 180 degrees Celsius.
2. In your big skillet, warm up half of oil on moderate temp. Put onions plus garlic then cook within three mins.
3. Put spinach to your skillet, then cook within two mins. Transfer it to your big container, then mix in ricotta, mozzarella, salt, plus pepper.
4. Stuff each portobello mushroom cap using spinach-ricotta mixture. Brush rest of oil onto each stuffed mushroom cap.
5. Put it in your cooking basket, then cook within fifteen mins till cheese is melted. Serve.

INGREDIENTS:

Four big portobello mushrooms, cleaned & scraped
200 grams spinach
250 grams ricotta cheese
100 grams mozzarella cheese, grated
10 grams minced garlic
50 grams chopped onion
30 millilitres olive oil
Salt & pepper, as required

NUTRITIONAL VALUES (PER SERVING): CALORIES: 330, CARBS: 8G, FAT: 25G, PROTEIN: 17G

INGREDIENTS:

500 grams peeled, sliced, boiled, strained & mashed potatoes
250 grams cabbage, shredded
150 grams bacon, chopped & cooked
100 grams chopped onion
Salt & pepper, as required
Oil spray

For the Apple Chutney:
300 grams apples, chopped
200 millilitres apple cider vinegar
100 grams brown sugar
Five millilitres cinnamon, ground

Bubble & Squeak
PATTIES WITH APPLE CHUTNEY

🕐 **PREP**: 15 min   🍲 **COOK**: 15 min   🍴 **SERVES**: 4

DIRECTIONS:

1. Put onion to your pan, cook till translucent, then add cabbage. Cook within five mins.
2. In your container, mix mashed potatoes, cabbage mixture, plus bacon. Flavour it using salt plus pepper.
3. Warm up your air fryer to 180 degrees Celsius. Oil your cooking basket using oil spray.
4. Shape prepared mixture into eight patties. Put them in your cooking basket, then cook within fifteen mins till golden brown, flipping once.
5. Mix apples, vinegar, sugar, plus cinnamon in your saucepan. Simmer within twenty mins on low temp, mixing often till it thickens. Serve.

NUTRITIONAL VALUES (PER SERVING): CALORIES: 350, CARBS: 57G, FAT: 12G, PROTEIN: 9G

Red Pepper &
HALLOUMI SKEWERS

⏲ **PREP**: 15 min   🍲 **COOK**: 10 min   🍴 **SERVES**: 4

DIRECTIONS:

1. Whisk oil, juice, oregano, salt, plus pepper in your container.
2. Thread halloumi cubes plus pepper squares onto skewers. Add them to marinade, then toss gently. Marinate within ten mins.
3. Warm up your air fryer to 180 degrees Celsius. Put skewers in your cooking basket.
4. Cook within ten mins till peppers are tender, turning once. Serve.

INGREDIENTS:

500 grams halloumi, cubes
400 grams red bell peppers, deseeded & chopped
200 millilitres olive oil
50 millilitres lemon juice
Two grams oregano, dried
Salt & pepper, as required

NUTRITIONAL VALUES (PER SERVING): CALORIES: 510, CARBS: 10G, FAT: 44G, PROTEIN: 23G

Stilton & Broccoli
QUICHE

⏲ **PREP**: 20 min   🍲 **COOK**: 25 min   🍴 **SERVES**: 6

DIRECTIONS:

1. Roll out shortcrust pastry, then line it in your oiled quiche dish. Refrigerate within fifteen mins.
2. Warm up your air fryer to 190 degrees Celsius. Parboil broccoli in boiling water within two mins, strain then put aside.
3. In your container, mix Stilton plus cheddar cheese.
4. In your separate container, whisk eggs plus double cream. Flavour it using salt plus pepper.
5. Take quiche dish, put broccoli in it, then sprinkle mixed cheeses on top. Pour egg mixture on top.
6. Put dish in your cooking basket, then cook within twenty-five mins till golden brown. Remove, cool it down, then serve.

INGREDIENTS:

200 grams shortcrust pastry
250 grams broccoli, chopped
100 grams Stilton cheese, crumbled
150 grams cheddar cheese, grated
Four eggs
300 millilitres double cream
Salt & pepper, as required

NUTRITIONAL VALUES (PER SERVING): CALORIES: 520, CARBS: 22G, FAT: 40G, PROTEIN: 21G

Goats Cheese & RED ONION TARTLETS

🕐 **PREP**: 15 min   🍲 **COOK**: 12 min   🍴 **SERVES**: 4

DIRECTIONS:

1. Warm up your air fryer to 180 degrees Celsius.
2. In your pan on moderate temp, cook onions in oil within five mins. Add balsamic vinegar, then cook within two mins. Flavour it using salt & pepper.
3. Put caramelized red onions in centre of each puff pastry square. Top each with goats' cheese. Fold edges towards centre to create a border.
4. Put tartlets into your cooking basket, then cook within twelve mins till golden brown. Serve.

INGREDIENTS:

200 grams puff pastry, rolled out & sliced into four
150 grams goats cheese, crumbled
Two medium sliced red onions
30 millilitres olive oil
30 millilitres balsamic vinegar
Salt & pepper, as required

NUTRITIONAL VALUES (PER SERVING): CALORIES: 485, CARBS: 35G, FAT: 33G, PROTEIN: 13G

Cheesy Cauliflower STEAKS

🕐 **PREP**: 10 min   🍲 **COOK**: 15 min   🍴 **SERVES**: 4

DIRECTIONS:

1. Warm up your air fryer to 180 degrees Celsius.
2. In your small container, mix oil, salt, plus pepper. Brush each cauliflower steak with it.
3. Put cauliflower steaks in your cooking basket. Cook within ten mins till steaks are tender.
4. In your separate container, mix cheddar, mozzarella, plus paprika. Sprinkle it on each cauliflower steak. Cook within five mins till cheese is melted.

INGREDIENTS:

One big cauliflower, sliced into steaks
30 millilitres olive oil
Two grams each salt & black pepper
50 grams grated each mozzarella & cheddar cheese
Four grams paprika

NUTRITIONAL VALUES (PER SERVING): CALORIES: 295, CARBS: 15G, FAT: 22G, PROTEIN: 12G

Wild Mushroom
& BRIE PIE

🕐 **PREP**: 20 min   🍲 **COOK**: 25 min   🍴 **SERVES**: 4

DIRECTIONS:

1. Warm up your air fryer to 200 degrees Celsius.
2. Toss mushrooms, oil, salt, plus pepper in your big container. Put mushrooms onto half of each pastry square. Top it using Brie cheese cubes. Fold each to seal.
3. Brush top of each pie using beaten egg. Put pies in your cooking basket, then cook within twenty-five mins till golden brown.

INGREDIENTS:

600 grams mixed wild mushrooms, sliced
200 grams Brie cheese, cubed
400 grams puff pastry, rolled out & sliced into four
One egg, beaten
50 millilitres olive oil
Salt & pepper, as required

NUTRITIONAL VALUES (PER SERVING): CALORIES: 670, CARBS: 51G, FAT: 46G, PROTEIN: 18G

Asparagus &
GRUYÈRE TART

🕐 **PREP**: 20 min   🍲 **COOK**: 25 min   🍴 **SERVES**: 6

DIRECTIONS:

1. Warm up your air fryer to 180 degrees Celsius.
2. Roll out puff pastry on your floured surface to form a rectangle.
3. Lay rolled-out puff pastry onto your lined baking sheet, then score a border around it.
4. Prick centre of your pastry dough, then spread Gruyère cheese. Put asparagus plus tomatoes on top.
5. In your small container, whisk egg plus milk, then brush it on pastry dough. Flavour it using salt plus pepper.
6. Cook in your cooking basket within twenty-five mins till crispy. Remove, cool it down, slice, then serve.

INGREDIENTS:

500 grams puff pastry
300 grams asparagus, trimmed
200 grams Gruyère cheese, grated
100 grams cherry tomatoes, halved
50 millilitres milk
50 grams beaten egg
Salt & pepper, as required

NUTRITIONAL VALUES (PER SERVING): CALORIES: 528, CARBS: 35G, FAT: 37G, PROTEIN: 16G

Cheddar & Leek POTATO CAKES

🕐 **PREP**: 20 min   🖳 **COOK**: 20 min   🍴 **SERVES**: 4

DIRECTIONS:

1. In your big pot, put potatoes plus water, then let it boil. Cook within ten mins till tender. Strain, cool it down, then mash in your big container. Mix in leeks, salt, pepper plus cheddar cheese.
2. Put flour on your plate, then put beaten egg in your shallow container. Shape it into eight patties. Coat them in flour, then dip into egg.
3. Warm up your air fryer to 200 degrees Celsius. Oil sprays your cooking basket.
4. Put patties in your cooking basket, then cook within ten mins. Flip, then cook within ten mins till crispy. Serve.

INGREDIENTS:

500 grams potatoes, peeled & diced
100 grams leeks, sliced
100 grams cheddar cheese, grated
50 grams flour, plain
One big egg, beaten
Salt & pepper, as required
Olive oil spray for air fryer

NUTRITIONAL VALUES (PER SERVING): CALORIES: 345, CARBS: 32G, FAT: 16G, PROTEIN: 15G

INGREDIENTS:

300 grams flour, all-purpose
150 grams cold butter, unsalted, diced
Five millilitres cold water
One kilogram mixed vegetables
200 grams cheddar cheese, grated
One litre vegetable stock
Salt & pepper, as required

Vegetable & Cheese PASTY

🕐 **PREP**: 15 min   🖳 **COOK**: 20 min   🍴 **SERVES**: 4

DIRECTIONS:

1. In your big container, mix flour plus butter till crumbly.
2. Add water, then mix till a dough forms. Wrap it in plastic wrap, then refrigerate within fifteen mins.
3. In your big container, mix vegetables, cheese, plus vegetable stock. Flavour it using salt plus pepper.
4. Warm up your air fryer to 180 degrees Celsius. Divide chilled dough into four, then roll each piece into a circle.
5. Put vegetable & cheese mixture in each dough circle. Fold dough, pinch edges to seal.
6. Put them in your cooking basket, then cook within twenty mins till golden brown.

NUTRITIONAL VALUES (PER SERVING): CALORIES: 680, CARBS: 68G, FAT: 35G, PROTEIN: 20G

Mushroom & Chestnut
WELLINGTON

⏱ **PREP**: 20 min   🍲 **COOK**: 30 min   🍴 **SERVES**: 4

DIRECTIONS:

1. Warm up your air fryer to 180 degrees Celsius.
2. In your pan on moderate temp, put oil, then cook onion plus garlic till softened. Put mushrooms, then cook till tender.
3. Mix in chestnuts, then flavour it using salt plus pepper. Cook within five mins, mixing often.
4. Put spinach, then cook till wilted. Remove mixture, then put aside. Unroll puff pastry onto your flat surface.
5. Spoon prepared mixture onto half of your pastry sheet. Fold remaining half of your pastry on filling, pressing to seal.
6. Transfer it to your cooking basket, then cook within thirty mins till pastry is crispy. Remove, cool it down, slice, then serve.

INGREDIENTS:

500 grams chestnut mushrooms, chopped
200 grams cooked & peeled chestnuts, chopped
One sheet vegan puff pastry, ready-rolled
100 grams baby spinach leaves
150 grams diced onion
Two cloves minced garlic
30 millilitres olive oil
Salt & pepper, as required

NUTRITIONAL VALUES (PER SERVING): CALORIES: 600, CARBS: 45G, FAT: 36G, PROTEIN: 14G

INGREDIENTS:

150 grams green lentils
500 grams mixed root vegetables, peeled & chopped
50 grams onion, chopped
Two garlic cloves, minced
500 millilitres vegetable stock
300 grams potatoes, peeled & chopped
100 millilitres almond milk, unsweetened
30 grams vegan butter
Salt & pepper, as required

Vegan Shepherd's Pie
WITH LENTILS & ROOT VEG

⏱ **PREP**: 20 min   🍲 **COOK**: 30 min   **SERVES**: 4

DIRECTIONS:

1. In your cooking basket, spread root vegetables. Cook within twenty mins till tender at 180 degrees Celsius.
2. In your medium saucepan, cook green lentils plus vegetable stock on moderate temp within fifteen mins till tender.
3. Meanwhile, in your big pan on moderate temp, dissolve half butter, then cook onion plus garlic till translucent.
4. Add cooked root vegetable, then mix well. Strain cooked lentils, then put them to your pan; Flavour it using salt plus pepper.
5. In your separate pot with boiling water, cook potatoes till tender. Strain, then mash with milk plus rest of butter; Flavour it using salt plus pepper.
6. Transfer vegetable-lentil mixture to your ovenproof dish. Top using mashed potatoes, then cook within fifteen mins till top is golden brown.

NUTRITIONAL VALUES (PER SERVING): CALORIES: 420, CARBS: 60G, FAT: 14G, PROTEIN: 18G

Falafel with
VEGAN TZATZIKI

🕐 **PREP**: 20 min   🍲 **COOK**: 15 min   🍴 **SERVES**: 4

DIRECTIONS:

1. Put chickpeas, onion, parsley, cilantro, garlic, cumin, coriander, paprika, salt plus pepper in your food processor. Pulse till slightly chunky. Form it into twelve patties.
2. Warm up your air fryer to 180 degrees Celsius. Brush each falafel patty using oil.
3. Put falafels in your cooking basket. Cook within fifteen mins till crispy.
4. Meanwhile, mix vegan yogurt, cucumber, garlic, dill, salt plus pepper in your small container. Serve falafels with vegan tzatziki.

INGREDIENTS:

400 grams canned chickpeas, strained & washed
100 grams chopped onion
50 grams chopped parsley & cilantro
Three minced cloves garlic
Ten grams ground cumin
Five grams ground coriander
Two grams paprika
Salt & black pepper, as required

30 millilitres olive oil

+ For the vegan tzatziki:
300 millilitres vegan yogurt, unsweetened
150 grams cucumber, grated & squeezed
One minced clove garlic
Ten grams dill, chopped
Salt & black pepper, as required

NUTRITIONAL VALUES (PER SERVING): CALORIES: 350, CARBS: 40G, FAT: 15G, PROTEIN: 14G

INGREDIENTS:

300 grams pressure-packed banana blossom
200 grams flour, wholemeal
500 grams potatoes, sliced into chips
250 millilitres sparkling water
100 grams panko breadcrumbs
50 millilitres vegetable oil
Salt & pepper, as required

Tartare Sauce:
150 millilitres vegan mayonnaise
30 grams capers, chopped
Two gherkins, finely diced
Fifteen millilitres lemon juice
Salt & pepper, as required

Vegan 'Fish' & Chips
WITH TARTARE SAUCE

🕐 **PREP**: 20 min   🍲 **COOK**: 25 min   🍴 **SERVES**: 4

DIRECTIONS:

1. Warm up your air fryer to 200 degrees Celsius.
2. Toss potatoes, oil plus salt. Cook in your cooking basket within twenty-five mins till crispy.
3. Mix flour, water, salt, plus pepper in your container. Coat banana blossom with it, then roll it in breadcrumbs.
4. Put them in your cooking basket, then spray using oil. Cook within twelve to fifteen mins till crispy.
5. For tartare sauce, mix mayonnaise, capers, gherkins, juice, plus salt and pepper in your small container.
6. Serve Vegan 'Fish' & Chips hot with tartare sauce.

NUTRITIONAL VALUES (PER SERVING): CALORIES: 535, CARBS: 78G, FAT: 19G, PROTEIN: 19G

Lentil & Vegetable
CURRY WITH AIR FRIED ROTI

🕐 **PREP**: 15 min   🍲 **COOK**: 30 min   🍴 **SERVES**: 4

DIRECTIONS:

1. In your big saucepan, warm up oil on moderate temp. Put onions, then cook till soft.
2. Put garlic and ginger, mixing within one min. Mix in curry powder.
3. Add lentils, broth, mixed vegetables, tomatoes, salt, plus pepper. Let it boil, adjust to low temp. Simmer within twenty-five mins till lentils are tender.
4. For roti dough, mix flour plus salt in your container. Mix in water till a dough forms. Knead within five mins.
5. Divide dough into eight, then roll each into a thin circle. Warm up your air fryer to 180 degrees Celsius.
6. Put roti in your cooking basket, then cook within two mins per side till puffed. Serve lentil & vegetable curry with cooked roti.

INGREDIENTS:

200 grams red lentils
One litre vegetable broth
300 grams mixed vegetables
200 grams canned tomatoes
100 grams onion, chopped
Two garlic minced cloves
Fifteen grams ginger, grated
Ten millilitres vegetable oil
Five grams curry powder
Salt & pepper, as required

+ For Roti:
250 grams flour, whole wheat
Five grams salt
150 millilitres water

NUTRITIONAL VALUES (PER SERVING): CALORIES: 453, CARBS: 77G, FAT: 5G, PROTEIN: 22G

Crispy Air Fried Tofu
WITH SWEET CHILLI DIP

🕐 **PREP**: 15 min   🍲 **COOK**: 20 min   🍴 **SERVES**: 4

DIRECTIONS:

1. Put cornstarch in your shallow container, then coat each tofu using it. Grease your cooking basket using oil.
2. Warm up your air fryer to 180 degrees Celsius.
3. Put coated tofu cubes in your cooking basket. Cook within twenty mins, turning once, till crispy.
4. Meanwhile, mix sweet chilli sauce, soy sauce, vinegar, plus coriander in your small container. Serve with cooked tofu.

INGREDIENTS:

400 grams firm tofu, strained, squeezed & sliced into cubes
30 grams cornstarch
One litre vegetable oil

+ Sweet Chilli Dip:
100 millilitres sweet chilli sauce
30 millilitres soy sauce
20 millilitres rice vinegar
Fifteen grams coriander, chopped

NUTRITIONAL VALUES (PER SERVING): CALORIES: 290, CARBS: 32G, FAT: 12G, PROTEIN: 16G

Eggplant & Tomato
GRATIN

🕐 **PREP**: 15 min   🍲 **COOK**: 20 min   🍴 **SERVES**: 4

DIRECTIONS:

1. Warm up your air fryer to 180 degrees Celsius.
2. In your big container, mix eggplant, half of oil, salt, plus pepper.
3. Put eggplant slices in your cooking basket, then cook within eight mins, flipping once.
4. In another container, mix breadcrumbs plus rest of oil.
5. In your gratin dish, layer eggplant plus tomato slices alternatively. Sprinkle each layer using cheese till all is used.
6. Spread breadcrumb mixture on top. Cook in your cooking basket within twelve mins. Serve.

INGREDIENTS:

500 grams eggplant, sliced
400 grams tomatoes, sliced
150 grams vegan cheese, grated
100 grams breadcrumbs
40 millilitres olive oil
Salt & pepper, as required

NUTRITIONAL VALUES (PER SERVING): CALORIES: 325, CARBS: 23G, FAT: 20G, PROTEIN: 13G

INGREDIENTS:

Four big bell peppers, sliced & seeded
200 grams quinoa, cooked
150 grams chopped onion
200 grams mixed vegetables
Five grams minced cloves garlic
400 millilitres vegetable broth
50 millilitres olive oil
Salt & pepper, as required

Stuffed Bell Peppers
WITH QUINOA & VEGETABLES

🕐 **PREP**: 15 min   🍲 **COOK**: 20 min   🍴 **SERVES**: 4

DIRECTIONS:

1. Warm up your air fryer to 180 degrees Celsius.
2. Warm up oil in your pan on moderate temp. Put onions plus garlic, then cook till tender.
3. Mix in vegetables, then cook within five mins. Mix in cooked quinoa, then flavour it using salt plus pepper.
4. Stuff each bell pepper using quinoa mixture. Put them in your cooking basket, then cook within twenty mins till peppers have softened.

NUTRITIONAL VALUES (PER SERVING): CALORIES: 380, CARBS: 55G, FAT: 12G, PROTEIN: 13G

Sweet Potato &
BLACK BEAN EMPANADASROTI

🕐 **PREP**: 30 min   🍲 **COOK**: 20 min   🍴 **SERVES**: 4

DIRECTIONS:

1. In your big pan, warm up oil on moderate temp. Put onion plus garlic, then cook within five mins.
2. Add sweet potatoes, bell pepper, cumin, paprika, salt, plus pepper. Cook within ten mins. Mix in black beans plus corn, then put aside.
3. Put sweet potato mixture onto each dough circle. Dab water along pastry edge, then fold it to cover fillings. Press down to seal.
4. Warm up your air fryer to 180 degrees Celsius.
5. Put empanadas into your cooking basket, then cook within twenty mins till golden brown, flipping once. Remove, cool it down, then serve.

INGREDIENTS:

200 grams sweet potatoes, peeled & diced
100 grams black beans, cooked & strained
One kilogram puff pastry, chilled, rolled out & sliced into twelve circles
100 grams chopped onion
150 grams red bell pepper, diced
50 grams frozen corn, thawed
Three garlic cloves, minced
Five millilitres olive oil
Two millilitres each ground cumin & paprika
Salt & pepper, as required
Water, as required

NUTRITIONAL VALUES (PER SERVING): CALORIES: 450, CARBS: 60G, FAT: 18G, PROTEIN: 12G

INGREDIENTS:

500 grams potatoes, peeled, chopped, boiled & strained
150 grams vegan cheese, grated
100 grams onion, chopped
200 grams frozen puff pastry, thawed, rolled out & sliced into four circles
30 millilitres plant milk, unsweetened
Salt & pepper, as required

Vegan Cheese &
ONION PIE

🕐 **PREP**: 15 min   🍲 **COOK**: 20 min   🍴 **SERVES**: 4

DIRECTIONS:

1. Mash potatoes, then add vegan cheese plus onion. Mix again, then put aside.
2. Warm up your air fryer to 200 degrees Celsius.
3. Divide potato mixture between pastry circles, fold, then press to seal. Brush milk on top of each.
4. Put them in your cooking basket, then cook within twenty mins till puffed up. Remove, cool it down, then serve.

NUTRITIONAL VALUES (PER SERVING): CALORIES: 425, CARBS: 52G, FAT: 22G, PROTEIN: 10G

Mediterranean Vegetable & OLIVE TART

🕐 **PREP**: 15 min   🍲 **COOK**: 20 min   🍴 **SERVES**: 4

DIRECTIONS:

1. Warm up your air fryer to 180 degrees Celsius. Put rolled out puff pastry to your cooking basket.
2. In your container, mix tomatoes, bell peppers, courgette, olives, plus oil. Flavour it using salt plus pepper.
3. Spread it on puff pastry, then cook within fifteen and crispy. Cool it down, slice, then serve.

INGREDIENTS:

300 grams puff pastry, rolled out
200 grams cherry tomatoes
100 grams each yellow & red bell pepper & courgette, sliced
50 grams black olives, halved & seeded
15 millilitres olive oil
Salt & pepper, as required

NUTRITIONAL VALUES (PER SERVING): CALORIES: 468, CARBS: 35G, FAT: 30G, PROTEIN: 12G

INGREDIENTS:

100 grams plain flour
200 millilitres almond milk
Three big eggs
Salt, as required
Five millilitres vegetable oil
300 grams canned jackfruit, strained & shredded
200 grams button mushrooms, sliced
One medium onion, diced
Ten millilitres olive oil
Salt & pepper, as required

Jackfruit & Mushroom STUFFED YORKSHIRE PUDDINGS

🕐 **PREP**: 20 min   🍲 **COOK**: 25 min   🍴 **SERVES**: 4

DIRECTIONS:

1. Whisk flour, milk, eggs, plus salt till smooth in your container. Put aside.
2. Warm up your air fryer to 200 degrees Celsius.
3. In your pan on moderate temp, warm up oil, then cook onion within five mins till softened.
4. Put mushrooms, then cook within five mins. Mix in jackfruit, then flavour it using salt plus pepper. Cook within five mins, then put aside.
5. Oil four pudding, then put them in your cooking basket within two mins. Remove warmed pudding tins, then pour Yorkshire pudding batter into each tin.
6. Spoon jackfruit-mushroom mixture into centre of each.
7. Put filled tins back into your cooking basket, then cook within twenty to twenty-five mins till puffed up. Remove, cool it down, then serve.

NUTRITIONAL VALUES (PER SERVING): CALORIES: 413, CARBS: 46G, FAT: 18G, PROTEIN: 14G

Vegan Sausage
ROLLS

🕐 **PREP**: 15 min   🍲 **COOK**: 20 min   🍴 **SERVES**: 4

DIRECTIONS:

1. Warm up your air fryer to 180 degrees Celsius.
2. Split vegan sausage meat alternative into four portions. Roll each into a cylinder shape, then put one on each pastry rectangle. Fold pastry to seal.
3. Brush each rolls using milk, then put in your cooking basket. Cook within twenty mins till crispy, turning once. Remove, cool it down, then serve.

INGREDIENTS:

200 grams vegan puff pastry, rolled out & sliced into four rectangles
200 grams vegan sausage meat alternative
50 millilitres almond milk, unsweetened

NUTRITIONAL VALUES (PER SERVING): CALORIES: 450, CARBS: 45G, FAT: 25G, PROTEIN: 10G

INGREDIENTS:

300 grams pasta of choice
200 grams fresh spinach
50 grams pine nuts
100 grams vegan Parmesan cheese, grated
Two garlic minced cloves
50 millilitres olive oil
500 millilitres vegan tomato sauce
Salt & pepper, as required

Vegan Spinach & Pine
NUT PESTO PASTA BAKE

🕐 **PREP**: 15 min   🍲 **COOK**: 20 min   🍴 **SERVES**: 4

DIRECTIONS:

1. Cook pasta in your skillet with boiling salted water till tender. Strain, then put aside.
2. Blend spinach, pine nuts, vegan Parmesan, garlic, plus oil till smooth in your food processor.
3. In your big container, mix cooked pasta plus spinach pesto. Warm up your air fryer to 180 degrees Celsius.
4. Spread tomato sauce layer in your baking dish. Add pesto pasta mix on top, then press down.
5. Pour rest of tomato sauce on pasta, then sprinkle rest of vegan parmesan.
6. Put dish in your cooking basket, then cook within twenty mins till pasta is golden. Remove, cool it down, then serve.

NUTRITIONAL VALUES (PER SERVING): CALORIES 450, CARBS 55G, FAT 20G, PROTEIN 15G

Roasted Vegetable
COUSCOUS BOWL

🕐 PREP: *15 min*   ▣ COOK: *20 min*   🍴 SERVES: *4*

DIRECTIONS:

1. Warm up your air fryer to 180 degrees Celsius.
2. In your big container, toss bell peppers, zucchini, onion, oil, salt, pepper, plus paprika.
3. Put seasoned vegetables in your cooking basket. Cook within twenty mins till slightly charred, shaking often.
4. Transfer it with couscous in your big container. Add cherry tomatoes, feta, plus parsley, then mix well. Serve.

INGREDIENTS:

200 grams bell peppers, deseeded & chopped
200 grams zucchini, sliced
200 grams red onion, chopped
500 grams cooked couscous, cooked
30 millilitres olive oil
Three grams each salt & black pepper
Two grams paprika
100 grams cherry tomatoes, halved
150 grams feta cheese, crumbled
50 grams parsley, chopped

NUTRITIONAL VALUES (PER SERVING): CALORIES: 510, CARBS: 67G, FAT: 21G, PROTEIN: 17G

Warm Potato &
GREEN BEAN SALAD

🕐 PREP: *15 min*   ▣ COOK: *25 min*   🍴 SERVES: *4*

DIRECTIONS:

1. Warm up your air fryer to 200 degrees Celsius.
2. In your container, toss potatoes, twenty millilitres oil, salt plus pepper.
3. Put potatoes in your cooking basket, then cook within twenty-five mins till golden brown, shaking once.
4. In your small container, whisk rest of oil, juice, garlic, salt, plus pepper.
5. In your big container, mix potatoes, green beans, tomatoes, onion, plus feta. Drizzle dressing on top, then slowly toss. Serve.

INGREDIENTS:

500 grams baby potatoes, halved
300 grams green beans, trimmed & boiled
80 millilitres olive oil
30 millilitres lemon juice
One garlic clove, minced
Salt & pepper, as required
200 grams cherry tomatoes, halved
50 grams red onion, thinly sliced
100 grams feta cheese, crumbled

NUTRITIONAL VALUES (PER SERVING): CALORIES: 362, CARBS: 34G, FAT: 21G, PROTEIN: 8G

Halloumi & Air Fried
MEDITERRANEAN VEG SALAD

🕐 **PREP**: 15 min   🍲 **COOK**: 20 min   🍴 **SERVES**: 4

DIRECTIONS:

1. Warm up your air fryer to 180 degrees Celsius.
2. In your big container, toss tomatoes, bell peppers, onion, courgettes, aubergine plus half of oil. Flavour it using salt plus pepper.
3. Put vegetables in your cooking basket, then cook within fifteen to twenty mins till tender, shaking once.
4. Meanwhile, warm up rest of oil in your non-stick skillet on moderate-high temp. Add halloumi, then cook within two to three mins per side.
5. Transfer vegetables to your big serving, then mix in lemon juice. Top it with cooked halloumi, then serve.

INGREDIENTS:

250 grams halloumi cheese, sliced
200 grams each cherry tomatoes & chopped bell peppers
150 grams sliced each red onion & courgette
200 grams aubergine, cubed
60 millilitres olive oil
Salt & pepper, as required
40 millilitres lemon juice

NUTRITIONAL VALUES (PER SERVING): CALORIES: 463, CARBS: 22G, FAT: 34G, PROTEIN: 18G

INGREDIENTS:

200 grams kale, washed & dried
200 grams apples, sliced
100 grams pecans, chopped
40 grams cranberries, dried
80 millilitres olive oil
40 millilitres lemon juice
Salt & pepper to taste

Crispy Kale &
APPLE SALAD

🕐 **PREP**: 10 min   🍲 **COOK**: 10 min   🍴 **SERVES**: 4

DIRECTIONS:

1. Warm up your air fryer to 180 degrees Celsius.
2. In your big container, toss kale, thirty millilitres oil, salt plus pepper.
3. Put kale in your cooking basket, then cook within five mins till crispy. Remove, then cool it down.
4. In your small container, whisk rest of oil plus juice till blended.
5. In your big container, mix kale, apple, pecans, plus cranberries. Add oil-lemon juice dressing, then toss slowly. Serve.

NUTRITIONAL VALUES (PER SERVING): CALORIES 400, CARBS 32G, FAT 28G, PROTEIN 5G

Sweet Potato &
FETA SALAD

🕐 **PREP**: 15 min   📟 **COOK**: 20 min   🍴 **SERVES**: 4

DIRECTIONS:

1. Warm up your air fryer to 180 degrees Celsius.
2. In your container, toss sweet potatoes, fifteen millilitres oil, salt plus pepper.
3. Put sweet potatoes in your cooking basket, then cook within twenty mins till crispy, shaking your basket once. Remove, then cool it down.
4. In your big container, mix salad greens, sweet potatoes, tomatoes, onion plus feta cheese.
5. In your small container, whisk rest of oil plus vinegar. Flavour it using salt plus pepper. Add it on salad, toss slowly. Serve.

INGREDIENTS:

600 grams sweet potatoes, diced
200 grams mixed salad greens
150 grams cherry tomatoes, halved
100 grams feta cheese, crumbled
50 grams red onion, thinly sliced
30 millilitres olive oil
Salt & pepper, as required
15 millilitres balsamic vinegar

NUTRITIONAL VALUES (PER SERVING): CALORIES: 410, CARBS: 50G, FAT: 20G, PROTEIN: 10G

INGREDIENTS:

400 grams broccoli florets
10 grams garlic, minced
200 grams quinoa, uncooked, washed & strained
One litre water
100 grams cherry tomatoes, halved
80 grams red onion, sliced
Four grams salt
Two grams black pepper
30 millilitres each lemon juice & olive oil

Roasted Broccoli &
QUINOA BOWL

🕐 **PREP**: 15 min   📟 **COOK**: 20 min   🍴 **SERVES**: 4

DIRECTIONS:

1. Warm up your air fryer to 200 degrees Celsius.
2. Mix broccoli, garlic plus fifteen millilitres oil in your big container. Flavour it using two grams salt plus one of black pepper.
3. Put it in your cooking basket, then cook within fifteen to twenty mins till tender, shaking your basket once.
4. In your medium saucepan, boil one litre water. Add quinoa, adjust to low temp, then simmer within twelve to fifteen mins till quinoa is tender. Fluff, then put aside to cool down.
5. In your big container, mix quinoa, broccoli, tomatoes, plus onion. Add rest of oil plus juice, then flavour it using salt plus pepper. Mix well, then serve.

NUTRITIONAL VALUES (PER SERVING): CALORIES: 325, CARBS: 47G, FAT: 11G, PROTEIN: 13G

Crispy Cauliflower &
TAHINI DRESSING SALAD

🕐 **PREP**: 10 min　　🍲 **COOK**: 15 min　　🍴 **SERVES**: 4

DIRECTIONS:

1. Warm up your air fryer to 200 degrees Celsius.
2. In your big container, mix cauliflower, oil, salt, plus pepper.
3. In your separate container, add breadcrumbs. Coat cauliflower in it, then put them in your cooking basket. Cook within fifteen mins till crispy, shaking once.
4. Meanwhile, mix tahini, juice, garlic, water, salt, plus pepper in your small container till smooth.
5. Pu mixed greens on your serving plate. Top with tomatoes plus cucumber. Put cooked cauliflower florets on top, then add tahini dressing. Serve.

INGREDIENTS:

One kilogram cauliflower florets
30 millilitres olive oil
Five grams salt
Three grams black pepper, ground
100 grams panko breadcrumbs

+ Tahini Dressing:
60 millilitres tahini
30 millilitres lemon juice

Two grams minced garlic
30 millilitres water
Salt & pepper, as required

+ For Salad:
200 grams mixed greens
200 grams cherry tomatoes, halved
100 grams cucumber, sliced

NUTRITIONAL VALUES (PER SERVING): CALORIES: 440, CARBS: 32G, FAT: 28G, PROTEIN: 14G

Air Fried Beetroot &
GOAT'S CHEESE SALAD

🕐 **PREP**: 15 min　　🍲 **COOK**: 20 min　　🍴 **SERVES**: 4

DIRECTIONS:

1. Warm up your air fryer to 180 degrees Celsius.
2. Toss beetroot, oil, salt, plus pepper. Put them in your cooking basket, then cook within twenty mins till tender.
3. In your big container, mix arugula, cooked beetroot, plus walnuts. Add oil plus vinegar, then toss slowly. Add goat cheese, salt plus pepper. Serve.

INGREDIENTS:

500 grams beetroot, peeled & chopped
250 grams goat's cheese, crumbled
100 grams each arugula & walnuts
50 millilitres each balsamic vinegar & olive oil
Salt & pepper, as required

NUTRITIONAL VALUES (PER SERVING): CALORIES: 490, CARBS: 18G, FAT: 37G, PROTEIN: 20G

Crispy Brussels
SPROUTS & PECAN SALAD

  PREP: 10 min   COOK: 15 min   SERVES: 4

DIRECTIONS:

1. Warm up your air fryer to 200 degrees Celsius.
2. In your container, mix Brussels sprouts, oil, salt, plus pepper. Put seasoned Brussels sprouts into your cooking basket.
3. Cook within fifteen mins till crispy, shaking once. Remove, then cool it down.
4. Meanwhile, mix pecans, Brussels sprouts, cranberries, blue cheese, plus mixed salad leaves in your big container.
5. In your small container, mix vinegar plus oil. Flavour it using salt plus pepper. Add dressing, then toss slowly. Serve.

INGREDIENTS:

500 grams Brussels sprouts, trimmed
and halved
30 millilitres olive oil
Salt & pepper, as required
150 grams pecans, roughly chopped
100 grams dried cranberries
100 grams blue cheese, crumbled
100 grams mixed salad leaves

For Dressing:
60 millilitres balsamic vinegar
120 millilitres olive oil
Salt & pepper, as required

NUTRITIONAL VALUES (PER SERVING): CALORIES: 720, CARBS: 42G, FAT: 56G, PROTEIN: 14G

INGREDIENTS:

500 grams asparagus spears, trimmed
Fifteen millilitres olive oil
One gram each salt & pepper
150 grams cherry tomatoes, halved
100 grams mixed salad leaves
50 grams parmesan cheese shavings
45 millilitres lemon juice
Half lemon, zested

Roasted Asparagus &
LEMON SALAD

PREP: 10 min   COOK: 8 min   SERVES: 4

DIRECTIONS:

1. Warm up your air fryer to 200 degrees Celsius.
2. In your container, mix asparagus, oil, salt, plus pepper. Transfer them to your cooking basket. Cook within eight mins till lightly browned. Remove, then cool it down.
3. Mix asparagus, salad leaves, tomatoes, plus parmesan in your big container.
4. In your small container, mix juice plus zest, then add it to your salad. Serve.

NUTRITIONAL VALUES (PER SERVING): CALORIES: 207, CARBS: 18G, FAT: 10G, PROTEIN: 11G

Warm Lentil Salad
WITH AIR FRIED CARROTS & FENNEL

🕐 **PREP**: 15 min   🍲 **COOK**: 25 min   🍴 **SERVES**: 4

DIRECTIONS:

1. In your big saucepan, add green lentils, water, plus salt. Let it boil on moderate-high temp.
2. Adjust to low temp, then simmer within twenty-five to thirty mins till lentils are tender. Strain.
3. Warm up your air fryer to 180 degrees Celsius.
4. In your container, mix carrots, fennel, oil, cumin, plus coriander. Spread it out in your cooking basket.
5. Cook vegetables within fifteen mins till slightly golden, shaking once.
6. Transfer it to your serving container. Add juice plus parsley, then toss slowly. Flavour it using salt plus pepper. Serve.

INGREDIENTS:

200 grams green lentils
One litre water
Two grams salt
300 grams carrots, peeled and sliced into thin rounds
200 grams fennel bulbs, thinly sliced
30 millilitres olive oil
Three grams ground each coriander & cumin
25 millilitres lemon juice
10 grams parsley, chopped
Salt & pepper, as required

NUTRITIONAL VALUES (PER SERVING): CALORIES: 310, CARBS: 45G, FAT: 9G, PROTEIN: 15G

INGREDIENTS:

600 grams pumpkin, peeled & cubes
30 millilitres olive oil
Salt & black pepper, as required
100 grams rocket salad
150 grams cherry tomatoes, halved
100 grams feta cheese, crumbled
30 millilitres balsamic glaze

Roasted Pumpkin &
ROCKET SALAD

🕐 **PREP**: 15 min   🍲 **COOK**: 20 min   🍴 **SERVES**: 4

DIRECTIONS:

1. Warm up your air fryer to 180 degrees Celsius.
2. In your big container, mix pumpkin, oil, salt plus pepper.
3. Put seasoned pumpkin cubes into your cooking basket, then cook within twenty mins, shaking once. Remove, then cool it down.
4. Mix pumpkin cubes, rocket plus cherry tomatoes in your big container. Top it using feta cheese. Add balsamic glaze, then serve.

NUTRITIONAL VALUES (PER SERVING): CALORIES: 280, CARBS: 19G, FAT: 18G, PROTEIN: 8G

Air Fried Mushroom &
SPINACH SALAD

🕐 **PREP**: 10 min 　　 🍲 **COOK**: 15 min 　　 🍴 **SERVES**: 4

DIRECTIONS:

1. Warm up your air fryer to 190 degrees Celsius.
2. In your big container, mix mushrooms, half of oil, salt plus pepper.
3. Put mushrooms in your cooking basket, then cook within ten to fifteen mins, shaking once, till crispy. Remove, then cool it down.
4. In another big container, mix mushrooms, spinach, tomatoes, plus feta cheese.
5. In your small container, whisk rest of oil, vinegar, salt plus pepper. Add it on salad, then toss slowly. Serve.

INGREDIENTS:

400 grams mushrooms, sliced
300 grams fresh spinach
150 grams cherry tomatoes, halved
100 grams feta cheese, crumbled
50 millilitres olive oil
30 millilitres balsamic vinegar
Salt & pepper, as required

NUTRITIONAL VALUES (PER SERVING): CALORIES: 280, CARBS: 8G, FAT: 22G, PROTEIN: 12G

Avocado & Air Fried
TORTILLA SALAD

🕐 **PREP**: 15 min 　　 🍲 **COOK**: 8 min 　　 🍴 **SERVES**: 4

DIRECTIONS:

1. Warm up your air fryer to 180 degrees Celsius.
2. In your big container, toss tortilla strips, oil plus salt.
3. Put them in your cooking basket, then cook within six to eight mins till crispy, shaking once.
4. In your big salad container, mix avocado, tomatoes, sweetcorn, black beans, plus onion. Add lime juice, salt plus pepper.
5. Add mixed salad leaves, then toss slowly. Add tortilla strips, then toss again. Serve.

INGREDIENTS:

200 grams tortilla strips
400 grams avocados, cubed
200 grams cherry tomatoes, halved
100 grams each sweetcorn & black beans
50 grams red onion, chopped
15 millilitres lime juice
100 grams mixed salad leaves
15 millilitres olive oil
Salt & pepper, as required

NUTRITIONAL VALUES (PER SERVING): CALORIES: 389, CARBS: 47G, FAT: 20G, PROTEIN: 9G

Roasted Cherry Tomato
& MOZZARELLA SALAD

🕐 **PREP:** 10 min   🍲 **COOK:** 6 min   🍴 **SERVES:** 4

DIRECTIONS:

1. Warm up your air fryer to 200 degrees Celsius.
2. In your container, mix tomatoes, oil, salt, plus pepper.
3. Put seasoned cherry tomatoes in your cooking basket, then cook within six mins, shaking once. Remove, then cool it down.
4. In your big container, mix tomatoes, salad greens, basil, plus mozzarella. Add balsamic glaze, then mix again. Serve.

INGREDIENTS:

400 grams cherry tomatoes
15 millilitres olive oil
Salt & pepper, as required
200 grams mozzarella, torn into pieces
50 grams fresh basil leaves
100 grams mixed salad greens
15 millilitres balsamic glaze

NUTRITIONAL VALUES (PER SERVING): CALORIES: 240, CARBS: 8G, FAT: 18G, PROTEIN: 11G

Warm Barley Salad
WITH AIR FRIED ROOT VEGETABLES

🕐 **PREP:** 15 min   🍲 **COOK:** 30 min   🍴 **SERVES:** 4

DIRECTIONS:

1. Mix pearl barley plus water in your saucepan. Let it boil, then adjust to a simmer. Cook within twenty-five to thirty mins till tender. Strain, then cool it down.
2. Meanwhile, mix root vegetables, half of oil, salt plus pepper.
3. Warm up your air fryer to 190 degrees Celsius. Spread vegetables in your cooking basket, then cook within fifteen mins till they're tender, shaking often.
4. In your big container, mix barley, vegetables, arugula, tomatoes, plus feta. Add rest of oil plus vinegar, tossing slowly.
5. Flavour it using salt plus pepper, then serve.

INGREDIENTS:

200 grams pearl barley, washed & strained
One litre water
300 grams root vegetables, peeled & diced
50 millilitres olive oil
Salt & pepper, as required
30 grams arugula
150 grams cherry tomatoes, halved
100 grams feta cheese, crumbled
30 millilitres balsamic vinegar

NUTRITIONAL VALUES (PER SERVING): CALORIES: 412, CARBS: 46G, FAT: 20G, PROTEIN: 12G

Pea & Air Fried
CRISPY SHALLOT SALAD

🕐 **PREP**: 15 min   🍲 **COOK**: 10 min   🍴 **SERVES**: 4

DIRECTIONS:

1. Warm up your air fryer to 180 degrees Celsius.
2. In your container, mix shallots, five millilitres oil, salt plus pepper.
3. Transfer it to your cooking basket, then cook within eight to ten mins till crispy, shaking once. Remove, then cool it down.
4. In your big container, mix shallots, rocket leaves plus cooled peas. Add rest of oil plus vinegar, then toss slowly. Top it using feta cheese, then serve.

INGREDIENTS:

200 grams fresh peas, boiled, strained & cooled
150 grams shallots, thinly sliced
80 grams rocket leaves
100 grams feta cheese, crumbled
15 millilitres olive oil
Five millilitres balsamic vinegar
Salt & pepper, as required

NUTRITIONAL VALUES (PER SERVING): CALORIES: 220, CARBS: 18G, FAT: 12G, PROTEIN: 9G

INGREDIENTS:

200 grams whole garlic cloves
500 grams butter beans, cooked & strained
150 grams cherry tomatoes, halved
100 grams mixed salad leaves
50 millilitres olive oil
20 millilitres lemon juice
Salt & pepper, as required

Roasted Garlic &
BUTTER BEAN SALAD

🕐 **PREP**: 15 min   🍲 **COOK**: 20 min   🍴 **SERVES**: 4

DIRECTIONS:

1. Warm up your air fryer to 180 degrees Celsius.
2. In your small container, mix garlic cloves, fifteen millilitres oil plus salt.
3. Put garlic cloves in your cooking basket, then cook within fifteen to twenty mins till golden brown. Remove, then cool it down.
4. Meanwhile, mix garlic cloves, butter beans, tomatoes, plus salad leaves in your big container.
5. In your small container, whisk rest of oil, juice, salt, plus pepper. Add it on salad, then mix slowly. Serve.

NUTRITIONAL VALUES (PER SERVING): CALORIES: 390, CARBS: 46G, FAT: 17G, PROTEIN: 12G

Crispy Tofu & ASIAN SLAW BOWL

🕐 **PREP**: 15 min   🍲 **COOK**: 12 min   🍴 **SERVES**: 4

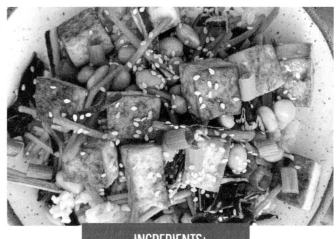

DIRECTIONS:

1. In your medium container, marinate tofu plus soy sauce within ten mins. Warm up your air fryer to 200 degrees Celsius.
2. Put marinated tofu in your cooking basket, then cook within twelve mins, shaking once.
3. In your big container, mix cabbages, carrots, green onions, plus cilantro.
4. In your small container, whisk vinegar, oil, plus lime juice. Add it to slaw, then mix well.
5. Top it using crispy tofu. Sprinkle with sesame seeds. Serve.

INGREDIENTS:

400 grams extra-firm tofu, strained & cubed
50 millilitres low-sodium soy sauce
200 grams shredded each red cabbage & green cabbage
100 grams shredded carrots
50 grams each sliced green onions & chopped cilantro
50 millilitres rice vinegar
25 millilitres each sesame oil & lime juice
10 grams toasted sesame seeds

NUTRITIONAL VALUES (PER SERVING): CALORIES: 295, CARBS: 25G, FAT: 15G, PROTEIN: 17G

INGREDIENTS:

400 grams canned chickpeas, strained & washed
600 grams aubergines, diced
60 millilitres olive oil
Two cloves garlic, minced
200 grams cherry tomatoes, halved
100 grams baby spinach
50 grams feta cheese, crumbled
30 millilitres balsamic vinegar
Salt & pepper, as required

Warm Chickpea & AIR FRIED AUBERGINE SALAD

🕐 **PREP**: 15 min   🍲 **COOK**: 20 min   🍴 **SERVES**: 4

DIRECTIONS:

1. Warm up your air fryer to 200 degrees Celsius.
2. In your big container, mix aubergines, two-thirds oil, garlic, salt, plus pepper.
3. Put coated aubergine in your cooking basket. Cook within ten to fifteen mins, shaking once, till aubergine are golden. Remove, then cool it down.
4. In your separate container, mix aubergine, chickpeas, tomatoes plus spinach.
5. Add rest of oil plus vinegar, then toss slowly. Top with feta, then serve.

NUTRITIONAL VALUES (PER SERVING): CALORIES: 352, CARBS: 42G, FAT: 17G, PROTEIN: 12G

Air Fried Butternut
SQUASH & POMEGRANATE SALAD

🕐 **PREP**: 15 min   📟 **COOK**: 25 min   🍴 **SERVES**: 4

DIRECTIONS:

1. Warm up your air fryer to 200 degrees Celsius.
2. In your big container, toss butternut squash, oil, salt, plus pepper.
3. Put seasoned butternut squash in your cooking basket, then cook within twenty to twenty-five mins, shaking often, till tender. Remove, then cool it down.
4. Meanwhile, mix oil, vinegar, salt, plus pepper in your small container.
5. In your big salad container, mix butternut squash, baby greens plus mint leaves. Add pomegranate plus feta, then slowly toss. Serve.

INGREDIENTS:

800 grams butternut squash, peeled & cubed
10 grams olive oil
One gram salt
0.5-gram black pepper
200 grams pomegranate seeds
100 grams feta cheese, crumbled
40 grams fresh mint leaves, chopped
200 grams mixed baby greens

For the Dressing:
50 millilitres olive oil
30 millilitres balsamic vinegar
0.5-gram each salt & black pepper

NUTRITIONAL VALUES (PER SERVING): CALORIES: 450, CARBS: 45G, FAT: 23G, PROTEIN: 9G

Crispy Potato &
DILL SALAD

🕐 **PREP**: 10 min   📟 **COOK**: 20 min   🍴 **SERVES**: 4

DIRECTIONS:

1. Warm up your air fryer to 200 degrees Celsius.
2. Mix potatoes, oil, salt, plus pepper in your big container.
3. Put potatoes in your cooking basket, then cook within twenty mins till crispy, shaking once. Remove, then cool it down.
4. In your another big container, mix potatoes, cucumber, tomatoes, dill, plus onion.
5. In your small container, mix yogurt plus juice. Add it on salad, then slowly toss. Serve.

INGREDIENTS:

500 grams baby potatoes, halved
30 millilitres olive oil
Salt & pepper, as required
200 grams cucumber, sliced
100 grams cherry tomatoes, halved
40 grams fresh dill, chopped
100 grams red onion, sliced
100 millilitres Greek yogurt
15 millilitres lemon juice

NUTRITIONAL VALUES (PER SERVING): CALORIES: 280, CARBS: 40G, FAT: 9G, PROTEIN: 8G

Air Fryer Roasted Red
PEPPER & COUSCOUS
SALAD

🕐 **PREP**: 15 min   🍱 **COOK**: 10 min   🍴 **SERVES**: 4

DIRECTIONS:

1. Warm up your air fryer to 200 degrees Celsius.
2. Put red pepper quarters in your cooking basket. Cook within ten mins, turning once, till slightly charred. Remove, cool it down, then chop it.
3. Meanwhile, put couscous in your heat-resistant container, then pour hot broth. Cover, then let it stand within five mins. Fluff couscous, then put aside.
4. In your big container, mix bell peppers, couscous, tomatoes, cucumber, plus feta cheese.
5. In your small container, whisk oil, juice, salt, plus pepper, then add it to salad. Mix well, then serve.

INGREDIENTS:

400 grams sliced into quarters red bell peppers
200 grams couscous
300 millilitres vegetable broth
150 grams cherry tomatoes, halved
100 grams cucumber, diced
70 grams crumbled feta cheese
40 millilitres olive oil
40 millilitres lemon juice
Salt & pepper, as required

NUTRITIONAL VALUES (PER SERVING): CALORIES: 455, CARBS: 53G, FAT: 22G, PROTEIN: 14G

INGREDIENTS:

200 grams corn kernels
400 grams canned black beans, strained & washed
150 grams cherry tomatoes, halved
100 grams red onion, chopped
50 grams cilantro, chopped
30 millilitres lime juice
30 millilitres olive oil
Salt & pepper, as required

Air Fried Corn &
BLACK BEAN SALAD

🕐 **PREP**: 15 min   🍱 **COOK**: 10 min   🍴 **SERVES**: 4

DIRECTIONS:

1. Warm up your air fryer to 200 degrees Celsius.
2. Mix corn, five millilitres oil, salt plus pepper in your container. Transfer it into your cooking basket.
3. Cook within ten mins till crispy, shaking once. Remove, then cool it down.
4. In your big container, mix cooked corn, beans, tomatoes, onion, plus cilantro.
5. In your small container, whisk juice plus rest of oil. Add it on salad, then toss slowly. Flavour it using salt plus pepper, then serve.

NUTRITIONAL VALUES (PER SERVING): CALORIES: 274, CARBS: 40G, FAT: 9G, PROTEIN: 12G

Air Fryer Eton
MESS PARFAIT

🕐 PREP: *20 min*   🍲 COOK: *10 min*   🍴 SERVES: *4*

DIRECTIONS:

1. Warm up your air fryer to 180 degrees Celsius.
2. Put meringue pieces in your cooking basket, then cook within five mins till golden brown. Remove, then cool it down.
3. Mix strawberries plus ten grams caster sugar in your medium container, then put aside.
4. Whip double cream, yogurt, rest of caster sugar, plus vanilla in your separate container till soft peaks form.
5. Layer each of four serving glasses using cream mixture, sugared strawberries, plus air-fried meringue pieces. Repeat layers till finish. Serve.

INGREDIENTS:

100 grams meringue pieces
300 grams strawberries, halved
200 grams double cream
100 grams Greek yogurt
20 grams caster sugar
1.5 millilitres vanilla extract

NUTRITIONAL VALUES (PER SERVING): CALORIES: 389, CARBS: 40G, FAT: 22G, PROTEIN: 6G

INGREDIENTS:

150 grams pitted dates, chopped
250 millilitres boiling water
Five grams baking soda
100 grams unsalted butter, softened
100 grams brown sugar
Two big eggs
150 grams self-raising flour, sifted
5 millilitres vanilla extract

For the Caramel Drizzle:
200 grams granulated sugar
100 grams unsalted butter, cubed
250 millilitres heavy cream
Five millilitres vanilla extract

Sticky Toffee Pudding
WITH CARAMEL DRIZZLE

🕐 PREP: *20 min*   🍲 COOK: *25 min*   🍴 SERVES: *6*

DIRECTIONS:

1. Mix dates, boiling water plus baking soda in your heatproof container. Put aside within ten mins.
2. Whisk butter plus brown sugar in your big container till fluffy. Beat in eggs, ensuring each egg is fully blended. Fold in flour plus vanilla. Mix in date mixture till blended.
3. Oil six individual ramekins, then split batter among them.
4. Warm up your air fryer to 180 degrees Celsius. Cook within twenty-five mins till firm. Remove, cool it down, then serve

For the Caramel Drizzle:
1. Dissolve sugar plus butter till smooth in your saucepan on moderate temp. Whisk in heavy cream while mixing, then put vanilla.
2. Cook on low temp within five-seven mins, mixing often till slightly thickened. Drizzle it over each cooled sticky toffee pudding, then serve.

NUTRITIONAL VALUES (PER SERVING): CALORIES: 650, CARBS: 85G, FAT: 32G, PROTEIN: 7G

Apple & Blackberry
CRUMBLE TARTS

🕐 **PREP**: 20 min   🗄 **COOK**: 15 min   🍴 **SERVES**: 4

DIRECTIONS:

1. In your container, mix apples plus blackberries.
2. In another container, mix flour plus butter till crumbly. Mix in oats plus sugar till blended.
3. Warm up your air fryer to 180 degrees Celsius. Divide fruit mixture amongst four pre-made tart shells.
4. Sprinkle crumble mixture on each top, pressing down gently. Put tarts in your cooking basket, then cook within fifteen mins till crisp. Remove, cool it down, then serve it with custard.

INGREDIENTS:

200 grams apples, peeled, cored & diced
100 grams blackberries
100 grams plain flour
75 grams butter, unsalted, chilled & cubed
50 grams rolled oats
50 grams caster sugar
Four (ten centimetres each) pre-made tart shells
Custard for serving

NUTRITIONAL VALUES (PER SERVING): CALORIES: 528, CARBS: 68G, FAT: 26G, PROTEIN: 6G

Air Fryer Bakewell
TART BITES

🕐 **PREP**: 15 min   🗄 **COOK**: 10 min   🍴 **SERVES**: 6

DIRECTIONS:

1. Mix flour plus butter in your container till crumbly. Add cold water, then till dough forms. Wrap dough, then chill within ten mins.
2. Warm up your air fryer to 180 degrees Celsius.
3. Roll out dough to quarter-inch thickness on your floured surface. Slice out twelve rounds, then put them into your air fryer-safe tart tray. Spoon raspberry jam into each tart base.
4. In another container, whisk butter plus caster sugar till fluffy. Mix in ground almonds. Mix in egg plus almond extract.
5. Spoon it on each tart, then sprinkle almonds on each tart bite. Put tart tray into your cooking basket, then cook within ten mins till set. Remove, cool it down, then serve.

INGREDIENTS:

150 grams flour, all-purpose
75 grams butter, cold & cubed
30 millilitres cold water
200 grams raspberry jam
100 grams almonds, ground
100 grams caster sugar
100 grams butter, softened
One big egg, beaten
Five millilitres almond extract
50 grams flaked almonds

NUTRITIONAL VALUES (PER SERVING): CALORIES: 315, CARBS: 34G, FAT: 17G, PROTEIN: 6G

Air Fryer Cherry & ALMOND CLAFOUTIS

🕐 **PREP**: 15 min   📠 **COOK**: 35 min   🍴 **SERVES**: 6

DIRECTIONS:

1. In your container, whisk caster sugar, flour, eggs, milk, plus almond extract till smooth. Grease your cooking basket using oil.
2. Pour ground almonds in your basket, then put cherries on top. Pour batter on top.
3. Warm up your air fryer to 160 degrees Celsius. Cook within thirty-five mins till set. Remove, then cool it down. Serve.

INGREDIENTS:

300 grams fresh cherries, pitted
100 grams caster sugar
100 grams plain flour
Three eggs
250 millilitres whole milk
20 millilitres almond extract
Salt, as required
Vegetable oil, as needed
50 grams almonds, ground

NUTRITIONAL VALUES (PER SERVING): CALORIES: 310, CARBS: 41G, FAT: 10G, PROTEIN: 9G

INGREDIENTS:

200 grams dark chocolate
100 grams each butter & caster sugar
Three big eggs
60 grams flour, all-purpose
150 grams raspberries

Chocolate & Raspberry FONDANT POTS

🕐 **PREP**: 15 min   📠 **COOK**: 12 min   🍴 **SERVES**: 4

DIRECTIONS:

1. Dissolve dark chocolate plus butter in your heatproof container on your saucepan with simmering water, mixing often till smooth. Put aside, then cool it down.
2. In your separate big container, whisk caster sugar plus eggs till blended. Pour chocolate mixture into it while mixing. Add flour, then fold it in.
3. Split it between four oiled ramekins. Add six raspberries on each ramekin. Split rest of chocolate mixture between your ramekins.
4. Warm up your air fryer to 180 degrees Celsius.
5. Put ramekins into your cooking basket, then cook within twelve mins till firm. Remove, then cool it down. Serve.

NUTRITIONAL VALUES (PER SERVING): CALORIES 560, CARBS 55G, FAT 36G, PROTEIN 8G

Crispy Churros with CHOCOLATE DIPPING SAUCE

🕐 **PREP**: 15 min   🍲 **COOK**: 8 min   🍴 **SERVES**: 4

DIRECTIONS:

1. Mix flour plus salt in your container. Put aside. Boil water plus butter in your saucepan. Remove.
2. Slowly add flour mixture, mixing till dough forms. Cool it down. Add eggs, then mix till blended.
3. Put churro dough to your piping bag. Warm up your air fryer to 200 degrees Celsius.
4. Pipe eight churros onto your cooking basket, then cook within eight mins till crispy.
5. In your shallow container, mix sugar plus cinnamon. Roll churros in it.

For the Chocolate Dipping Sauce:
1. In your heatproof container set on your saucepan with simmering water, dissolve chocolate plus double cream, mixing often till smooth. Serve with churros.

INGREDIENTS:

200 grams flour, all-purpose
One gram salt
250 millilitres water
50 grams unsalted butter, melted
Two big eggs
20 grams sugar, granulated
One gram cinnamon, ground

For the Chocolate Dipping Sauce:
100 grams dark chocolate, broken into pieces
100 millilitres double cream

NUTRITIONAL VALUES (PER SERVING): CALORIES: 585, CARBS: 70G, FAT: 29G, PROTEIN: 11G

Treacle Tart WITH CLOTTED CREAM

🕐 **PREP**: 15 min   🍲 **COOK**: 25 min   🍴 **SERVES**: 8

DIRECTIONS:

1. Warm up your air fryer to 180 degrees Celsius. Line your air fryer-safe tart pan using rolled out pastry.
2. In your container, mix golden syrup, breadcrumbs, butter, egg, zest, plus ground ginger. Pour it into your pastry-lined tart pan.
3. Put tart pan in your cooking basket, then cook within twenty-five mins till filling is set. Remove, then cool it down. Serve treacle tart slices with clotted cream.

INGREDIENTS:

500 grams sweet shortcrust pastry, rolled out
300 grams golden syrup
100 grams breadcrumbs
75 grams butter, unsalted, dissolved
50 millilitres beaten egg
Zest of one lemon
Ground ginger, as required
To serve: clotted cream

NUTRITIONAL VALUES (PER SERVING): CALORIES: 541, CARBS: 72G, FAT: 26G, PROTEIN: 6G

Bread & Butter PUDDING BITES

🕐 **PREP**: *15 min* 📠 **COOK**: *15 min* 🍴 **SERVES**: *6*

DIRECTIONS:

1. In your big container, mix bread cubes plus milk. Let it soak within ten mins.
2. In your another container, mix butter, sugar, eggs, raisins, vanilla, cinnamon, plus nutmeg. Pour it on bread cubes, then gently mix.
3. Warm up your air fryer to 180 degrees Celsius. Grease your cooking basket. Scoop bread pudding mixture onto it.
4. Cook within fifteen mins till golden brown. Remove, cool it down, then serve.

INGREDIENTS:

150 grams bread, small cubes
200 millilitres milk
50 grams butter, unsalted, dissolved
50 grams sugar, granulated
Two beaten eggs
75 grams raisins
Five millilitres vanilla extract, pure
Ground cinnamon & nutmeg, as required

NUTRITIONAL VALUES (PER SERVING): CALORIES: 279, CARBS: 35G, FAT: 13G, PROTEIN: 6G

Lemon & Poppy SEED DRIZZLE CAKE

🕐 **PREP**: *15 min* 📠 **COOK**: *25 min* 🍴 **SERVES**: *8*

DIRECTIONS:

1. In your big container, mix flour, caster sugar, butter, eggs, plus milk. Beat till smooth. Fold in zest plus poppy seeds.
2. Grease your air fryer-safe cake pan, then add batter into it.
3. Warm up your air fryer to 160 degrees Celsius. Put cake pan into your cooking basket then cook within twenty-five mins. Remove, then cool it down.
4. Meanwhile, mix icing sugar plus juice in your small container. Remove cake, then put it on your serving plate. Add lemon on top. Serve.

INGREDIENTS:

225 grams flour, self-raising
175 grams caster sugar
175 grams butter, softened
Three big eggs
75 millilitres milk
Zest of two lemons
10 grams poppy seeds

For the drizzle:
80 grams icing sugar
One lemon, juiced

NUTRITIONAL VALUES (PER SERVING): CALORIES 396, CARBS 53G, FAT 18G, PROTEIN 5G

Mini Victoria
SPONGE CAKES

🕐 **PREP**: 15 min   📟 **COOK**: 12 min   🍴 **SERVES**: 4

DIRECTIONS:

1. In your container, whisk butter plus caster sugar till fluffy. Add eggs, then mix till blended. Sift in flour, then fold slowly.
2. Warm up your air fryer to 180 degrees Celsius. Oil four small ramekins using butter.
3. Split cake mixture between your ramekins. Put them in your cooking basket, cook within twelve mins till golden brown. Remove, cool it down, then slice each cake horizontally into two layers.
4. Spread jam on one layer, then spread double cream on another layer. Put some strawberry on your cream layer. Put jam-covered layer on top, dust using icing sugar. Serve.

INGREDIENTS:

100 grams flour, self-raising
100 grams butter, unsalted, softened
100 grams caster sugar
Two big eggs, beaten
One-eight kilograms halved strawberries
50 millilitres double cream, whipped
50 grams icing sugar
25 grams raspberry jam, seedless

NUTRITIONAL VALUES (PER SERVING): CALORIES: 475, CARBS: 60G, FAT: 24G, PROTEIN: 6G

Pear & Frangipane
TARTS

🕐 **PREP**: 20 min   📟 **COOK**: 20 min   🍴 **SERVES**: 6

DIRECTIONS:

1. Mix flour plus butter in your big container till crumbly.
2. Mix in granulated sugar, then mix in egg yolk plus water. Form dough into a ball, wrap, then refrigerate within ten mins.
3. Mix ground almonds, caster sugar, butter plus egg in another container. Warm up your air fryer to 180 degrees Celsius.
4. Roll out dough on your floured surface, then slice out six circles. Press each circle into your tart tin, then divide filling mixture among your six tarts.
5. Put pear slices on top of each, pressing gently. Put tarts into your lined cooking basket, then cook within twenty mins till filling is set.
6. Remove, cool it down, then dust using icing sugar. Serve.

INGREDIENTS:

200 grams flour, all-purpose
100 grams butter, unsalted, cold & cubed
50 grams sugar, granulated
One big egg yolk
30 millilitres water, ice-cold
75 grams almonds, ground
75 grams each caster sugar & softened butter
One big egg, beaten
Three ripe pears, cored & sliced
Icing sugar, as needed

NUTRITIONAL VALUES (PER SERVING): CALORIES: 520, CARBS: 60G, FAT: 30G, PROTEIN: 8G

Chocolate Eclairs with
VANILLA CREAM FILLING

🕐 **PREP**: 30 min   🍲 **COOK**: 20 min   🍴 **SERVES**: 8

DIRECTIONS:

1. Warm up your air fryer to 190 degrees Celsius.
2. Boil water, butter, plus salt in your medium saucepan. Add flour, then mix till it forms a ball. Remove, then cool it down.
3. Mix in eggs slowly, then transfer dough into your piping bag. Pipe eight éclairs onto your lined baking tray.
4. Cook in your cooking basket within twenty mins till golden brown. Cool it down.
5. Mis milk plus half of sugar in your medium saucepan, then let it simmer on moderate temp.
6. Whisk egg yolks, cornstarch, plus res of sugar in your separate container. Slowly whisk milk mixture into yolk mixture.
7. Strain into your saucepan, then cook, whisking till it thickens. Remove, then mix in vanilla. Cool it down, then put in your fridge to chill.
8. Put chopped chocolate in your container.
9. Warm up heavy cream in your saucepan, then pour on chocolate. Let it sit within one min, then mix till smooth.
10. Slice tops off each cooled éclair, then fill using vanilla cream. Spread chocolate glaze on each éclair. Serve.

INGREDIENTS:

120 millilitres water
60 grams butter, unsalted
One gram salt
75 grams flour, all-purpose
Three big eggs

For the vanilla cream filling:
480 millilitres whole milk
100 grams sugar, granulated

25 grams cornstarch
Three big egg yolks
Two grams vanilla extract, pure

For the chocolate glaze:
200 grams dark chocolate, chopped
120 millilitres heavy cream

NUTRITIONAL VALUES (PER SERVING): CALORIES: 460, CARBS: 48G, FAT: 25G, PROTEIN: 9G

INGREDIENTS:

200 grams digestive biscuits, crushed
100 grams butter, unsalted, dissolved
300 millilitres heavy whipping cream
One-litre caramel sauce
Three big bananas, sliced
50 grams dark chocolate shavings for garnish

Air Fried Banoffee
PIE CUPS

🕐 **PREP**: 15 min   🍲 **COOK**: 8 min   🍴 **SERVES**: 6

DIRECTIONS:

1. Mix digestive biscuits plus butter in your container till crumbly. Press it into your six silicone cupcake moulds.
2. Warm up your air fryer to 180 degrees Celsius.
3. Put moulds in your cooking basket, then cook within eight mins till golden brown. Remove, then cool it down.
4. In your separate container, whip heavy cream till soft peaks. Fill each cooled pie cup using caramel sauce, then add banana on top.
5. Top each using whipped cream, then sprinkle chocolate shavings. Serve.

NUTRITIONAL VALUES (PER SERVING): CALORIES 674, CARBS 73G, FAT 39G, PROTEIN 7G

Rhubarb & Custard
PASTRIES

🕐 **PREP**: 15 min   🍲 **COOK**: 10 min   🍴 **SERVES**: 4

DIRECTIONS:

1. Mix rhubarb plus sugar in your saucepan. Cook on moderate temp within five mins, till rhubarb is soft. Remove, then cool it down.
2. Warm up your air fryer to 190 degrees Celsius.
3. Roll out puff pastry into a 30cm x 30cm big square on your lightly floured surface. Slice pastry into four squares.
4. Spoon custard onto half of each pastry square. Top using rhubarb mixture. Fold pastry squares over, then press to seal.
5. Put pastries in your cooking basket, then cook within ten mins till puffed up. Remove, cool it down, then serve.

INGREDIENTS:

200 grams rhubarb, chopped
100 grams caster sugar
250 grams puff pastry, ready-made
150 millilitres custard, ready-made

NUTRITIONAL VALUES (PER SERVING): CALORIES: 450, CARBS: 63G, FAT: 19G, PROTEIN: 7G

INGREDIENTS:

100 grams ladyfinger biscuits
250 grams mascarpone cheese
100 millilitres brewed coffee, strong
50 millilitres coffee liqueur
200 millilitres heavy whipping cream
50 grams sugar, granulated
20 grams cocoa powder, unsweetened
100 grams dark chocolate, grated

Tiramisu
TRIFLE JARS

🕐 **PREP**: 15 min   🍲 **COOK**: 10 min   🍴 **SERVES**: 4

DIRECTIONS:

1. Mix brewed coffee plus coffee liqueur in your shallow container. Dip each ladyfinger biscuit in it.
2. Break moistened ladyfingers into small pieces, then put into four jars.
3. Whisk mascarpone, heavy cream, plus sugar in your container till blended. Spoon mascarpone mixture on ladyfingers.
4. Dust each using cocoa powder. Repeat steps for another layer in each jar. Warm up your air fryer to 160 degrees Celsius.
5. Put trifle jars in your cooking basket, then cook within ten mins till slightly warmed. Remove, then cool it down.
6. Decorate each trifle jar using dark chocolate. Serve.

NUTRITIONAL VALUES (PER SERVING): CALORIES: 640, CARBS: 46G, FAT: 45G, PROTEIN: 11G

Crispy Coconut
MACAROONS WITH CHOCOLATE DIP

🕐 **PREP**: 15 min   🍲 **COOK**: 10 min   🍴 **SERVES**: 20

DIRECTIONS:

1. Mix desiccated coconut, caster sugar, plus egg whites in your big container.
2. Warm up your air fryer to 160 degrees Celsius.
3. Shape coconut mixture into twenty small balls, then put them onto your lined cooking basket.
4. Cook within ten mins till golden brown. Remove, then cool it down.
5. Meanwhile, warm up double cream in your saucepan on low temp till it starts to simmer. Remove, then mix in dark chocolate till smooth.
6. Gently dip half of each macaroon into chocolate dip, then serve.

INGREDIENTS:

200 grams desiccated coconut, sweetened
80 grams caster sugar
100 grams egg whites
50 millilitres double cream
200 grams dark chocolate, chopped

NUTRITIONAL VALUES (PER SERVING): CALORIES: 140, CARBS: 11G, FAT: 9G, PROTEIN: 2G

Ginger & Golden
SYRUP STEAMED PUDDING

🕐 **PREP**: 20 min   🍲 **COOK**: 40 min   🍴 **SERVES**: 6

DIRECTIONS:

1. Mix flour plus butter till crumbly in your big container. Add sugar, eggs, ginger, syrup, plus milk. Mix till smooth.
2. Oil your heatproof baking dish using butter. Pour batter into your baking dish, then cover.
3. Warm up your air fryer to 160 degrees Celsius. Put covered baking dish in your cooking basket, then cook within forty mins till firm. Remove, cool it down, then serve.

INGREDIENTS:

250 grams flour, self-raising
150 grams butter, unsalted, softened
150 grams dark brown sugar
Three big eggs
100 grams crystallised ginger, chopped
60 millilitres golden syrup
40 millilitres milk

NUTRITIONAL VALUES (PER SERVING): CALORIES: 575, CARBS: 83G, FAT: 25G, PROTEIN: 8G

Black Forest
GATEAU POTS

🕐 **PREP**: 25 min   🍲 **COOK**: 15 min   🍴 **SERVES**: 4

DIRECTIONS:

1. Mix cherries, sugar, kirsch, plus water in your small saucepan. Simmer within ten mins till thickened. Put aside.
2. Dissolve dark chocolate till smooth in your microwave-safe container. Put aside.
3. Whip heavy cream using your stand mixer till soft peaks form. Split half chocolate sponge cake among ramekins.
4. Layer cherry syrup, whipped cream plus dark chocolate on each ramekin. Add chocolate sponge cake among your ramekins.
5. Top each again using cherry syrup, whipped cream, plus dark chocolate. Warm up your air fryer to 160 degrees Celsius.
6. Put ramekins in your cooking basket, then cook within fifteen mins till warmed. Remove, cool it down, then serve.

INGREDIENTS:

200 grams chocolate sponge cake, crumbled
150 grams dark chocolate, chopped
200 grams cherries, pitted & halved
250 millilitres heavy cream
100 grams sugar
50 millilitres each kirsch & water

NUTRITIONAL VALUES (PER SERVING): CALORIES: 680, CARBS: 69G, FAT: 42G, PROTEIN: 7G

INGREDIENTS:

200 grams butter, unsalted, softened
200 grams sugar, granulated
One big orange, zested
100 grams each polenta & ground almonds
Two big eggs, beaten
50 millilitres orange juice

Orange & Polenta
CAKE BITES

🕐 **PREP**: 15 min   🍲 **COOK**: 10 min   🍴 **SERVES**: 12

DIRECTIONS:

1. Whisk butter plus sugar till fluffy in your big container. Mix in zest, polenta, plus almonds till blended. Add eggs, mixing slowly till blended. Mix in juice till smooth.
2. Warm up your air fryer to 180 degrees Celsius. Split out twelve cake bites onto your baking paper. Transfer it into your cooking basket.
3. Cook within ten mins till firm. Remove, cool it down, then serve.

NUTRITIONAL VALUES (PER SERVING): CALORIES: 270, CARBS: 20G, FAT: 19G, PROTEIN: 4G

Spotted Dick &
VANILLA CUSTARD

🕐 **PREP**: 15 min   ▣ **COOK**: 25 min   🍴 **SERVES**: 4

DIRECTIONS:

1. Mix flour plus salt in your container. Rub butter in it till crumbly. Mix in sugar, currants, plus zest.
2. Mix in egg, then slowly add milk to form a soft dough. Shape it into a rectangular loaf on your parchment paper, then put into your cooking basket.
3. Cook at 180 degrees Celsius within twenty-five mins till golden brown.
4. Meanwhile, mix milk, vanilla pod and seeds in your saucepan till steaming.
5. In your separate container, whisk egg yolks, sugar, plus cornflour till smooth. Slowly pour hot milk on egg mixture while mixing for eggs to temper.
6. Pour mixture into your saucepan, then cook on low temp while mixing till thickened. Strain. Serve.

INGREDIENTS:

200 grams flour, self-raising
100 grams butter, unsalted, cold & cubed
50 grams sugar, granulated
100 grams currants
One lemon, zested
One egg, beaten
100 millilitres milk
Salt, as required

For the Vanilla Custard:
500 millilitres whole milk
One vanilla pod, split & scraped
Four egg yolks
75 grams sugar, granulated
25 grams cornflour

NUTRITIONAL VALUES (PER SERVING): CALORIES: 410, CARBS: 62G, FAT: 17G, PROTEIN: 15G

Mini Pavlovas with
SEASONAL FRUITS

🕐 **PREP**: 20 min   ▣ **COOK**: 60 min   🍴 **SERVES**: 6

DIRECTIONS:

1. Warm up your air fryer to 100 degrees Celsius.
2. Whisk egg whites in your big container till soft peaks form. Slowly add caster sugar plus cream of tartar, then whisk till glossy. Fold in vanilla.
3. Spoon six pavlova mixture onto your lined cooking basket. Cook within sixty mins till pavlovas are crisp. Remove, then cool it down.
4. Whip heavy cream in your chilled container till soft peaks form. Decorate each pavlova using whipped cream plus seasonal fruits.

INGREDIENTS:

120 grams egg whites
200 grams caster sugar
Two grams cream of tartar
Five millilitres pure vanilla extract
200 millilitres heavy cream
300 grams seasonal fruits

NUTRITIONAL VALUES (PER SERVING): CALORIES: 389, CARBS: 48G, FAT: 19G, PROTEIN: 5G

Bramley Apple Turnovers
WITH CINNAMON SUGAR

🕐 **PREP**: 15 min   🍱 **COOK**: 12 min   🍴 **SERVES**: 6

DIRECTIONS:

1. Mix apples, sugar, cinnamon, plus juice in your medium container. Put aside.
2. Put apple mixture onto half of each circle, then brush edges using egg wash. Fold in half to seal, then press it down.
3. Warm up your air fryer to 180 degrees Celsius.
4. Brush each turnover using egg wash, then make two small slits on top. Cook within twelve mins till golden brown. Remove, then cool it down. Serve.

INGREDIENTS:

300 grams puff pastry, rolled out & sliced into twelve circles
400 grams Bramley apples, peeled & diced
40 grams sugar, granulated
2 grams cinnamon
25 millilitres lemon juice
Egg wash, as required

NUTRITIONAL VALUES (PER SERVING): CALORIES: 450, CARBS: 49G, FAT: 25G, PROTEIN: 5G

Lancashire Eccles
CAKES

🕐 **PREP**: 15 min   🍱 **COOK**: 12 min   🍴 **SERVES**: 6

DIRECTIONS:

1. Warm up your air fryer to 190 degrees Celsius.
2. Mix butter, demerara sugar, currants, candied peel, mixed spice, zest, plus salt in your container till blended.
3. Put filling in centre of each dough circle. Moisten dough edges using water, then fold pastry, sealing well. Press it down, then brush each cake using milk.
4. Put cakes in your cooking basket within twelve mins till crisp. Remove, then cool it down. Serve.

INGREDIENTS:

225 grams puff pastry, rolled out & sliced into six circles
100 grams butter, unsalted, dissolved
100 grams demerara sugar
150 grams currants
50 grams candied peel, chopped
One-gram mixed spice
One lemon, zested
Salt, as required
30 millilitres milk for glazing

NUTRITIONAL VALUES (PER SERVING): CALORIES: 497, CARBS: 64G, FAT: 2G, PROTEIN: 7G

Jam Roly-Poly
WITH ENGLISH CUSTARD

🕐 **PREP**: 10 min   🍲 **COOK**: 25 min   🍴 **SERVES**: 4

DIRECTIONS:

1. Mix flour plus suet in your big container. Slowly add water, then mix till a soft dough form.
2. Flour your surface, then roll it out into a rectangular shape. Spread raspberry jam on dough.
3. Roll up your dough tightly, then pinch ends to seal. Wrap roly-poly in foil, then twist ends to secure.
4. Put roly-poly in your cooking basket, then cook at 180 degrees Celsius within twenty-five mins till golden brown.
5. Meanwhile, mix milk plus heavy cream in your saucepan on low temp till warm.
6. In your separate container, whisk egg yolks plus sugar, then slowly pour milk mixture, mixing.
7. Add it to your saucepan, then cook on low temp, mixing till it thickens. Remove, cool it down, unwrap roly-poly, then slice into four.
8. Drizzle each roly-poly slice using English custard. Serve.

INGREDIENTS:

200 grams flour, self-raising
100 grams suet
125 millilitres cold water
100 grams raspberry jam
125 millilitres milk
125 millilitres heavy cream
Three egg yolks
50 grams sugar, granulated

NUTRITIONAL VALUES (PER SERVING): CALORIES: 685, CARBS: 80G, FAT: 35G, PROTEIN: 14G

Argentinian Beef &
OLIVE EMPANADAS
(SOUTH AMERICAN)

🕐 **PREP**: 30 min   🍲 **COOK**: 16 min   🍴 **SERVES**: 4-6

DIRECTIONS:

1. Warm up oil, then cook onions till soft in your big pan.
2. Add ground beef, then cook till browned. Flavour it using salt plus pepper.
3. Mix in tomato sauce, vinegar, plus olives. Cook within five mins, remove, then cool it down.
4. Spoon beef filling onto half of each pastry circle. Fold to cover filling, then press edges to seal.
5. Warm up your air fryer to 180 degrees Celsius. Put empanadas in your cooking basket.
6. Cook within fifteen mins till golden brown, turning once. Serve.

INGREDIENTS:

500g beef, ground
300g puff pastry, rolled out & sliced into four to six circles
150g diced onion
120g green olives, chopped
100ml vegetable oil
50ml tomato sauce
30ml vinegar
Salt & pepper, as required

NUTRITIONAL VALUES (PER SERVING): CALORIES: 852, CARBS: 63G, FAT: 54G, PROTEIN: 27G

Oriental Congee with
SHIITAKE MUSHROOMS (ORIENTAL)

🕐 **PREP**: 15 min   📟 **COOK**: 45 min   🍴 **SERVES**: 4

DIRECTIONS:

1. Mix rice plus water in your big container. Put aside within ten mins.
2. Warm up your air fryer at 130 degrees Celsius. Transfer softened rice mixture to your baking dish.
3. Add mushrooms, ginger, soy sauce, oil, salt, plus white pepper. Mix well.
4. Put baking dish in your cooking basket. Cook within forty-five mins. Remove, then let it stand within five mins. Serve.

INGREDIENTS:

200 grams Jasmine rice, washed & strained
1.5-litres water
200 grams Shiitake mushrooms, sliced
Two grams ginger, minced
30 millilitres soy sauce
Five millilitres sesame oil
Salt & white pepper, as required

NUTRITIONAL VALUES (PER SERVING): CALORIES: 266, CARBS: 48G, FAT: 3G, PROTEIN: 10G

Shakshuka with Feta
& OLIVES (MEDITERRANEAN)

🕐 **PREP**: 10 min   📟 **COOK**: 15 min   🍴 **SERVES**: 4

DIRECTIONS:

1. Mix tomatoes, bell peppers, onion, plus garlic in your big container. Mix in cumin, paprika, plus cayenne pepper. Flavour it using salt plus pepper.
2. Warm up your air fryer to 180 degrees Celsius. Pour tomato-vegetable mixture into your greased cooking basket.
3. Cook within ten mins till vegetables are softened.
4. Make four holes in cooked vegetable mixture. Add egg into each hole. Cook within five mins. Remove, then top using feta plus black olives. Serve.

INGREDIENTS:

400 grams chopped tomatoes, canned
1 kg bell peppers, diced
200 grams white onion, chopped
20 grams garlic cloves, minced
10 millilitres olive oil
50 grams black olives, chopped
100 grams crumbled feta cheese
Four big eggs
Five grams each ground cumin & paprika
Two grams cayenne pepper
Salt & pepper, as required

NUTRITIONAL VALUES (PER SERVING): CALORIES: 290, CARBS: 18G, FAT: 18G, PROTEIN: 15G

Turkish Menemen
WITH AIR FRIED VEGETABLES (MEDITERRANEAN)

🕐 **PREP**: 15 min   📱 **COOK**: 25 min   🍴 **SERVES**: 4

DIRECTIONS:

1. Warm up your air fryer to 180 degrees Celsius.
2. Mix tomatoes, bell peppers, onion plus half of oil in your big container. Transfer it to your cooking basket, then cook within fifteen mins, shaking once.
3. Meanwhile, warm up rest of oil in your big skillet on moderate temp.
4. Add tomato paste, cumin and paprika, then cook within two mins. Mix in cooked vegetables. Make four holes in it, then add egg into each hole.
5. Cover, then cook within five mins till eggs are cooked. Remove, then sprinkle using feta. Flavour it using salt plus pepper. Serve.

INGREDIENTS:

400 grams tomatoes, chopped
200 grams each chopped green & red bell pepper
150 grams onion, chopped
Four big eggs
100 grams feta cheese, crumbled
50 millilitres olive oil
30 grams tomato paste
Five grams ground each cumin & paprika
Salt & pepper, as required

NUTRITIONAL VALUES (PER SERVING): CALORIES: 350, CARBS: 22G, FAT: 23G, PROTEIN: 14G

INGREDIENTS:

400 grams flour, all-purpose
200 millilitres warm water
6 grams instant yeast
60 grams white sugar
50 millilitres whole milk
100 grams powdered custard
50 grams butter, unsalted, softened
300 millilitres condensed milk, sweetened

Chinese Steamed
CUSTARD BUNS (ORIENTAL)

🕐 **PREP**: 15 min   📱 **COOK**: 15 min   🍴 **SERVES**: 4

DIRECTIONS:

1. Mix flour, warm water, instant yeast, sugar, plus milk in your big container to form a soft dough.
2. Knead it within ten mins till smooth. Cover, then let it rest within one hour.
3. Meanwhile, in another container, mix powdered custard, butter, plus condensed milk till smooth, then put aside.
4. Split it into twelve, roll each into a ball shape, then flatten it.
5. Spoon custard filling into centre of your flattened dough. Take up dough edges, then pinch them to seal. Put each filled bun on your small baking paper.
6. Warm up your air fryer to 180 degrees Celsius. Put buns on your lined cooking basket
7. Cook buns at 180 degrees Celsius within fifteen mins till golden brown. Remove, cool it down, then serve.

NUTRITIONAL VALUES (PER SERVING): CALORIES: 356, FAT: 57G, FAT: 12G, PROTEIN: 8G

Venezuelan Arepas with
AVOCADO & BLACK BEANS
(SOUTH AMERICAN)

🕐 **PREP**: 20 min   🍱 **COOK**: 20 min   🍴 **SERVES**: 4

DIRECTIONS:

1. Mix flour plus salt in your big container. Slowly pour warm water, then mix till a soft dough form. Let it rest within five mins.
2. Meanwhile, mix black beans, avocado, onion, cilantro, juice, salt plus pepper in your separate container.
3. Split dough into four, then shape each into a round disc. Warm up your air fryer to 180 degrees Celsius. Brush each arepa disc using oil.
4. Put arepas into your cooking basket, then cook within ten mins per side till crispy. Remove, then cool it down.
5. Slice each arepa in half horizontally to create a pocket. Stuff each arepa pocket using avocado-black bean filling. Serve.

INGREDIENTS:

250 grams arepa flour
500 millilitres warm water
3 grams salt
30 millilitres vegetable oil
400 grams canned black beans, strained & washed
One ripe avocado, diced
100 grams red onion, chopped
50 grams cilantro, chopped
30 millilitres lime juice
Salt & pepper, as required

NUTRITIONAL VALUES (PER SERVING): CALORIES: 458, CARBS: 63G, FAT: 20G, PROTEIN: 13G

Edamame with Sea
SALT & CHILI FLAKES
(ORIENTAL)

🕐 **PREP**: 10 min   🍱 **COOK**: 8 min   🍴 **SERVES**: 4

DIRECTIONS:

1. Warm up your air fryer to 200 degrees Celsius.
2. Mix edamame, oil, sea salt, plus chili flakes in your big container. Transfer it to your cooking basket.
3. Cook within eight min, shaking your basket once. Remove, then cool it down. Serve.

INGREDIENTS:

500 grams edamame
Fifteen millilitres olive oil
Five grams sea salt
Two grams chili flakes

NUTRITIONAL VALUES (PER SERVING): CALORIES: 150, CARBS: 8G, FAT: 9G, PROTEIN: 12G

Tapenade & Roasted
RED PEPPER CROSTINI
(MEDITERRANEAN)

🕐 **PREP:** 10 min   🍲 **COOK:** 8 min   🍴 **SERVES:** 4

DIRECTIONS:

1. Mix olives, red peppers, capers, garlic, juice, plus millilitres oil in your food processor. Process till chunky, then put aside.
2. Warm up your air fryer to 180 degrees Celsius. Brush ciabatta slices using oil.
3. Put ciabatta slices in your cooking basket, then cook within four mins per side till crispy. Remove, then cool it down.
4. Spread tapenade mixture onto each crostini slice. Flavour it using salt plus pepper. Serve.

INGREDIENTS:

200 grams ciabatta bread, sliced into one cm thick pieces
100 grams pitted black olives
100 grams roasted red peppers, strained & chopped
50 grams capers, strained
Two cloves garlic, peeled & chopped
30 millilitres lemon juice
60 millilitres olive oil
Salt & black pepper, as required

NUTRITIONAL VALUES (PER SERVING): CALORIES: 342, CARBS: 32G, FAT: 21G, PROTEIN: 6G

INGREDIENTS:

400 grams spinach, chopped
200 grams feta cheese, crumbled
100 grams green onions, chopped
One-litre boiling water
100 millilitres olive oil
Two minced cloves garlic
Two eggs, beaten
300 grams filo pastry sheets

Greek Spanakopita with
SPINACH & FETA
(MEDITERRANEAN)

🕐 **PREP:** 15 min   🍲 **COOK:** 20 min   🍴 **SERVES:** 4

DIRECTIONS:

1. Pour boiling water on spinach to wilt it in your big container. Strain, then cool it down.
2. Mix feta, green onions, garlic, plus eggs in another container. Add cooled spinach, then mix well.
3. Warm up your air fryer to 180 degrees Celsius.
4. Slice each filo pastry sheet into four rectangles, then brush one side of each rectangle using oil. Put spinach-feta mixture on one corner of each rectangle.
5. Fold pastry diagonally to form a triangle shape. Continue folding till its finish. Tuck any rest of pastry under itself to seal.
6. Put triangles in your cooking basket. Cook within twenty mins till crispy. Serve.

NUTRITIONAL VALUES (PER SERVING): CALORIES: 620, CARBS: 45G, FAT: 38G, PROTEIN: 22G

Vietnamese Vegetable
SPRING ROLLS (ORIENTAL)

🕐 **PREP**: 30 min   📠 **COOK**: 10 min   🍴 **SERVES**: 4

DIRECTIONS:

1. Put mixed vegetables, rice noodles, plus herbs in your damp rice paper centre.
2. Fold in rice paper sides on filling first. Fold in bottom edge, then roll it up to secure. Do same using rest of fixings.
3. Warm up your air fryer to 190 degrees Celsius. Coat each spring roll using oil.
4. Put spring rolls in your cooking basket, then cook within five mins per side till crispy. Remove, then cool it down. Serve.

INGREDIENTS:

Sixteen rice paper sheets, dip in water, & lay them flat on your work surface
300 grams mixed vegetables
100 grams rice noodles, cooked & strained
30 grams each basil & mint leaves
20 grams cilantro leaves

NUTRITIONAL VALUES (PER SERVING): CALORIES: 310, CARBS: 56G, FAT: 4G, PROTEIN: 9G

Brazilian Pão
DE QUEIJO
(SOUTH AMERICAN)

🕐 **PREP**: 15 min   📠 **COOK**: 20 min   🍴 **SERVES**: 4

DIRECTIONS:

1. Mix flour, Parmesan, plus cheddar cheese in your big container.
2. Mix milk, oil, plus salt in your small saucepan on moderate temp. Warm it up, then remove.
3. Pour hot milk mixture into cheese mixture, mixing till blended. Cool it down, then add egg. Mix till a smooth dough form.
4. Split dough into eight, then roll each one into a ball. Warm up your air fryer to 200 degrees Celsius.
5. put dough balls in your cooking basket, then cook within twenty mins till crispy. Remove, cool it down, then serve.

INGREDIENTS:

60 grams tapioca flour
30 grams grated each Parmesan & cheddar cheese
120 millilitres milk
50 millilitres vegetable oil
Salt, as required
One egg

NUTRITIONAL VALUES (PER SERVING): CALORIES: 241, CARBS: 24G, FAT: 12G, PROTEIN: 7G

Thai Mango &
PAPAYA SALAD (ORIENTAL)

🕐 **PREP**: 15 min   🍲 **COOK**: 10 min   🍴 **SERVES**: 4

DIRECTIONS:

1. Warm up your air fryer to 180 degrees Celsius.
2. Mix papaya, mango, tomatoes, cilantro, mint, plus garlic in your big container.
3. Mix fish sauce, juice, plus honey in your small container. Add it on papaya-mango mixture, then toss slowly.
4. Put it in your cooking basket. Cook within ten mins till warmed, shaking every five mins. Remove, then top it using peanuts. Serve.

INGREDIENTS:

One-kilogram green papaya, peeled & shredded
300 grams mango, peeled & julienned
150 grams cherry tomatoes, halved
75 grams peanuts, unsalted, roasted
50 grams each chopped cilantro & mint leaves
Four minced cloves garlic
80 millilitres each fish sauce & lime juice
30 millilitres honey

NUTRITIONAL VALUES (PER SERVING): CALORIES: 300, CARBS: 45G, FAT: 9G, PROTEIN: 10G

INGREDIENTS:

200 grams orzo pasta
One-kilogram mixed Mediterranean vegetables
Two minced cloves garlic
30 millilitres olive oil
Salt & pepper, as required
50 grams black olives, sliced
100 grams feta cheese, cubed
30 grams basil leaves, chopped
15 millilitres balsamic vinegar

Mediterranean Orzo
& ROASTED VEG SALAD
(MEDITERRANEAN)

🕐 **PREP**: 20 min   🍲 **COOK**: 25 min   🍴 **SERVES**: 4

DIRECTIONS:

1. Warm up your air fryer to 200 degrees Celsius. Cook orzo pasta in your skillet with water till tender. Strain, then put aside.
2. Toss it with vegetables, garlic, oil, salt, plus pepper in your big container. Move it in your cooking basket. Cook within twenty mins, shaking once.
3. Mix cooked orzo plus vegetables in your big container. Put olives, feta, basil leaves plus vinegar, then mix well. Serve.

NUTRITIONAL VALUES (PER SERVING): CALORIES: 539, CARBS: 67G, FAT: 22G, PROTEIN: 18G

Moroccan Chickpea &
COUSCOUS BOWL (MEDITERRANEAN)

🕐 **PREP:** 15 min   ▣ **COOK:** 20 min   🍴 **SERVES:** 4

DIRECTIONS:

1. Warm up your air fryer to 180 degrees Celsius.
2. Mix chickpeas, oil, cumin, paprika, cinnamon, salt, plus pepper in your big container.
3. Put seasoned chickpeas in your cooking basket, then cook within fifteen mins, shaking once.
4. Meanwhile, cook couscous using boiling water in your skillet till tender. Fluff, then put aside in your big container.
5. Mix in chickpeas, tomatoes, olives, plus bell pepper. Serve.

INGREDIENTS:

200 grams dried couscous
400 grams canned chickpeas, strained & washed
100 grams cherry tomatoes, halved
50 grams Kalamata olives, chopped
200 grams red bell pepper, chopped
30 millilitres olive oil
Two grams ground each cumin & paprika
One gram cinnamon, ground
Salt & pepper, as required

NUTRITIONAL VALUES (PER SERVING): CALORIES 420, CARBS 65G, FAT 12G, PROTEIN 14G

INGREDIENTS:

200 grams flour, all-purpose
400 grams kimchi, chopped
150 grams scallions, chopped
2 cloves garlic, minced
50 grams ginger, grated
200 millilitres cold water
Salt, as required

Korean Kimchi
PANCAKES (ORIENTAL)

🕐 **PREP:** 15 min   ▣ **COOK:** 12 min   🍴 **SERVES:** 4

DIRECTIONS:

1. Mix flour, kimchi, scallions, garlic plus ginger in your big container.
2. Slowly pour cold water, mixing till smooth. Flavour it using salt.
3. Warm up your air fryer to 190 degrees Celsius. Grease your cooking basket using oil spray.
4. Spoon enough batter into your cooking basket. Cook within six mins per side till crisp. Do same using your rest of batter. Serve.

NUTRITIONAL VALUES (PER SERVING): CALORIES: 360, CARBS: 60G, FAT: 5G, PROTEIN: 15G

Teriyaki Salmon & ASIAN GREENS (ORIENTAL)

🕐 PREP: 15 min   🍲 COOK: 10 min   🍴 SERVES: 4

DIRECTIONS:

1. Marinate salmon in teriyaki sauce within ten mins. Warm up your air fryer to 200 degrees Celsius.
2. Take marinated salmon, then put in your cooking basket. Cook within eight to ten mins till cooked.
3. Toss Asian greens, oil, soy sauce, garlic, salt, plus pepper in your big container. Spread seasoned greens around your salmon during last three mins.
4. Remove, plate the decorate sesame on top. Serve.

INGREDIENTS:

600 grams salmon fillet, sliced into four
200 millilitres teriyaki sauce
300 grams Asian greens, mixed
15 grams sesame seeds
20 millilitres each olive oil & soy sauce
Five grams garlic, minced
Salt & pepper, as required

NUTRITIONAL VALUES (PER SERVING): CALORIES: 450, CARBS: 8G, FAT: 28G, PROTEIN: 40G

INGREDIENTS:

200 grams each diced eggplant, bell pepper & zucchini
200 grams cherry tomatoes, halved
One small red onion, chopped
Two cloves garlic, minced
15 millilitres olive oil
Two grams basil, dried
One gram oregano, dried
Salt & pepper, as required

For the crispy polenta:
500 millilitres water
100 grams instant polenta
30 millilitres olive oil
Salt & pepper, as required

Ratatouille with Crispy Polenta (MEDITERRANEAN STYLE)

🕐 PREP: 20 min   🍲 COOK: 40 min   🍴 SERVES: 6

DIRECTIONS:

1. Mix eggplant, zucchini, bell pepper, tomatoes, onion, garlic, oil, basil, oregano, salt plus pepper in your big container.
2. Warm up your air fryer to 180 degrees Celsius.
3. Pour vegetable mixture into your cooking basket, then cook within twenty-five mins, shaking once.
4. Boil water in your medium saucepan. Pour polenta while mixing. Cook within five mins on low temp till it thickens. Flavour it using salt plus pepper.
5. Spread it on your lined baking tray, then cool it down. Adjust your air fryer temperature to 200 degrees Celsius.
6. Slice cooled polenta into squares, then brush using oil.
7. Put polenta pieces in your cooking basket, then cook within fifteen mins, flipping once, till crispy. Serve ratatouille on crispy polenta squares.

NUTRITIONAL VALUES (PER SERVING): CALORIES: 350, CARBS: 50G, FAT: 12G, PROTEIN: 7G

Spanish Paella with
MEDITERRANEAN VEGETABLES

🕐 **PREP:** 20 min   🍲 **COOK:** 40 min   🍴 **SERVES:** 4

DIRECTIONS:

1. Warm up your air fryer to 190 degrees Celsius.
2. Put onion, bell peppers, plus zucchini in your container. Mix in fifteen millilitres cooking oi.
3. Transfer it to your cooking basket, then cook within fifteen mins, mixing often.
4. Warm up fifteen millilitres oil in your big pan on moderate temp. Add Arborio rice, then toast within three mins, mixing.
5. Add saffron plus paprika, then mix within one min. Pour broth, let it boil, then adjust to low temp. Simmer within twenty mins till tender.
6. Meanwhile, add thawed seafood to your cooked vegetables. Cook within five mins at 190 degrees Celsius till warmed.
7. Mix cooked rice, vegetables, plus seafood in your big serving container. Flavour it using salt. Serve.

INGREDIENTS:

200 grams Arborio rice
500 millilitres vegetable broth
100 grams diced each onion, bell pepper (yellow & red) & zucchini
150 grams canned tomatoes, strained & chopped
300 grams mixed seafood
One litre cooking oil

For Spices:
One-gram saffron threads
Two grams smoked paprika
Salt, as required

NUTRITIONAL VALUES (PER SERVING): CALORIES: 477, CARBS: 54G, FAT: 10G, PROTEIN: 34G

Thai Green Curry
WITH CRISPY TOFU (ORIENTAL)

🕐 **PREP:** 20 min   🍲 **COOK:** 20 min   🍴 **SERVES:** 4

DIRECTIONS:

1. Warm up your air fryer to 180 degrees Celsius.
2. Mix tofu plus oil in your big container. Put them in your cooking basket, then cook within ten mins, turning once.
3. Meanwhile, add Thai green curry paste then cook within two mins in your big pan on moderate temp.
4. Add coconut milk, then let it boil. Adjust to a simmer within ten mins. Add sugar snap peas plus baby corn. Simmer within five mins.
5. Fold crispy tofu in it. Add lime juice plus soy sauce, then serve on cooked rice.

INGREDIENTS:

400 grams firm tofu, strained & cubed
15 millilitres vegetable oil
50 grams Thai green curry paste
400 millilitres coconut milk
200 grams sugar snap peas, trimmed
200 grams baby corn, halved lengthwise
15 millilitres each lime juice & soy sauce
One-kilogram cooked jasmine rice

NUTRITIONAL VALUES (PER SERVING): CALORIES: 658, CARBS: 90G, FAT: 25G, PROTEIN: 27G

Peruvian Lomo
SALTADO (SOUTH AMERICAN)

🕐 **PREP**: 15 min   🍲 **COOK**: 20 min   🍴 **SERVES**: 4

DIRECTIONS:

1. Warm up your air fryer to 190 degrees Celsius.
2. Mix potatoes, five millilitres oil plus salt. put them in your cooking basket, then cook within fifteen to twenty mins, shaking often till crispy.
3. Meanwhile, mix beef strips, five millilitres oil, soy sauce, vinegar, cumin, salt, plus pepper in your big container. Marinate within five mins.
4. Warm up your pan on moderate-high temp with rest of oil. Add beef strips, then cook within three to four mins till browned. Remove beef, then put aside.
5. Cook onions within two mins in your same pan till tender. Add tomatoes, then cook within one min while mixing. Add cooked beef, then mix well.
6. Add cooked fries, then mix slowly. Serve.

INGREDIENTS:

400 grams beef sirloin, thin strips
600 grams potatoes, sliced into fries
100 grams each sliced red onion & halved cherry tomatoes
40 millilitres each soy sauce & red wine vinegar
20 grams cilantro, chopped
Two grams ground cumin
Salt & pepper, as required
15 millilitres vegetable oil

NUTRITIONAL VALUES (PER SERVING): CALORIES: 587, CARBS: 45G, FAT: 18G, PROTEIN: 40G

Chilean Porotos
GRANADOS (SOUTH AMERICAN)

🕐 **PREP**: 20 min   🍲 **COOK**: 40 min   🍴 **SERVES**: 4

DIRECTIONS:

1. Put beans plus one litre water in your saucepan. Bring to a boil then cook within forty mins, or till tender. Strain, then put aside.
2. Warm up your air fryer to 180 degrees Celsius.
3. Mix pumpkin plus two millilitres oil in your big container. Flavour it using salt plus pepper.
4. Transfer it to your cooking basket, then cook within fifteen mins. Put aside.
5. Warm up eight millilitres oil in your big saucepan on moderate temp. Add onion plus garlic, then cook till softened.
6. Mix in beans, corn, plus tomatoes within five mins. Add half litre broth, then simmer within fifteen mins on low temp.
7. Fold in cooked pumpkin within five mins. Serve hot.

INGREDIENTS:

200 grams dried, soaked overnight & washed white beans
500 grams pumpkin, cubed
200 grams corn kernel
100 grams onion, chopped
Two garlic cloves, minced
200 grams tomatoes, canned, diced
Half litre vegetable broth
One litre water
Ten millilitres olive oil
Salt & pepper, as required

NUTRITIONAL VALUES (PER SERVING): CALORIES: 330, CARBS: 53G, FAT: 6G, PROTEIN: 18G

Japanese Agedashi
TOFU (ORIENTAL)

🕐 **PREP**: 15 min   🍲 **COOK**: 20 min   🍴 **SERVES**: 4

DIRECTIONS:

1. Warm up your air fryer to 180 degrees Celsius.
2. Roll each tofu in potato starch. Grease your cooking basket using oil.
3. Put coated tofu in it, then cook within eighteen to twenty mins, turning them once, till crispy. Remove onto serving container.
4. Mix dashi, mirin, plus soy sauce in your small saucepan, then warm it up on moderate temp.
5. Pour warm sauce on tofu, then decorate spring onions plus bonito flakes on top. Serve.

INGREDIENTS:

400 grams firm tofu, strained & sliced into eight
60 grams potato starch
500 millilitres vegetable oil
80 millilitres dashi
30 millilitres mirin
20 millilitres soy sauce
Two sliced spring onions
Eight grams bonito flakes

NUTRITIONAL VALUES (PER SERVING): CALORIES: 290, CARBS: 20G, FAT: 16G, PROTEIN: 20G

Greek Moussaka with
LENTILS & AUBERGINES
(MEDITERRANEAN)

🕐 **PREP**: 20 min   🍲 **COOK**: 40 min   🍴 **SERVES**: 6

DIRECTIONS:

1. Add lentils plus water in your medium saucepan, let it boil, then adjust to a simmer within twenty mins till tender. Strain, then put aside.
2. Warm up your air fryer to 200 degrees Celsius. Brush each aubergine using oil, then cook in your cooking basket within eight mins per side till golden. Put aside.
3. Cook onions plus garlic in your big skillet on moderate temp with rest of oil within five mins till softened.
4. Add tomatoes, tomato paste, lentils, salt, pepper, cinnamon, plus nutmeg. Cook within ten mins on low temp.
5. Warm up your oven to 180 degrees Celsius.
6. Dissolve butter in your saucepan on low temp.
7. Add flour, then mix till smooth. Slowly pour milk, whisking till it thickens. Cook within five mins on low temp. Flavour it using salt, pepper, plus nutmeg.
8. Layer cooked aubergines, plus lentil mixture in your rectangular baking dish.
9. Add béchamel sauce on top, then bake within thirty-five or till golden. Remove, cool it down, then serve.

INGREDIENTS:

150 grams green lentils
One litre water
Two large aubergines, sliced into one-cm thick rounds
50 millilitres olive oil
One big onion, chopped
Two cloves garlic, minced
200 grams chopped tomatoes, canned
25 grams tomato paste
Salt & pepper, as required
Two grams cinnamon, ground
Two grams nutmeg, ground

For the béchamel sauce:
50 grams butter, unsalted
50 grams flour, plain
600 millilitres milk
Salt, pepper, & nutmeg, as required

NUTRITIONAL VALUES (PER SERVING): CALORIES: 410, CARBS: 44G, FAT: 19G, PROTEIN: 18G

Falafel & Tzatziki
WRAP (MEDITERRANEAN)

🕐 **PREP**: 20 min　　🍲 **COOK**: 15 min　　🍴 **SERVES**: 4

DIRECTIONS:

1. Add chickpeas, onion, parsley, cilantro, cumin, coriander, salt, pepper plus garlic in your food processor. Process till blended. Mix in baking soda.
2. Form it into sixteen small balls, then flatten them. Warm up your air fryer to 200 degrees Celsius.
3. Put falafels in your cooking basket, then cook within fifteen mins till crispy.
4. Mix tzatziki sauce fixings in your container. Put four falafels in each wrap, then add tzatziki sauce on top. Serve.

INGREDIENTS:

200 grams dried chickpeas, soaked overnight
100 grams onion, chopped
Fifteen grams chopped each parsley & cilantro
Three grams ground each cumin & coriander
Two grams salt
One-gram black pepper
Five grams garlic, minced
Two grams baking soda
30 millilitres olive oil

For Tzatziki Sauce:
300 millilitres Greek yogurt, plain
100 grams cucumber, grated & strained
20 millilitres lemon juice
Two grams salt
One-gram black pepper
Five grams garlic, minced

To serve:
Four big wraps, whole wheat, warmed

NUTRITIONAL VALUES (PER SERVING): CALORIES: 595, CARBS: 65G, FAT: 24G, PROTEIN: 30G

Chinese Vegetable
LO MEIN (ORIENTAL)

🕐 **PREP**: 15 min　　🍲 **COOK**: 15 min　　🍴 **SERVES**: 4

DIRECTIONS:

1. Warm up your air fryer to 180 degrees Celsius.
2. In your big container, mix carrots, bell peppers, bean sprouts, mushrooms, oil plus garlic.
3. Transfer it to your cooking basket, then cook within ten mins till tender, shaking once.
4. In your small container, whisk soy & oyster sauce, sesame oil, plus cornstarch.
5. Mix cooked noodles plus vegetables in your big pan on moderate temp. Add sauce, then toss slowly till warmed. Serve.

INGREDIENTS:

300 grams uncooked noodles, cooked & strained
150 grams each julienned carrots & bean sprouts
200 grams sliced bell peppers
100 grams sliced mushrooms
Two cloves garlic, minced
20 millilitres vegetable oil
60 millilitres soy sauce
30 millilitres oyster sauce
Ten millilitres sesame oil
Five grams cornstarch

NUTRITIONAL VALUES (PER SERVING): CALORIES: 372, CARBS: 52G, FAT: 12G, PROTEIN: 12G

Asian Slaw with
PEANUT DRESSING
(ORIENTAL)

🕐 **PREP**: 15 min   📟 **COOK**: 10 min   🍴 **SERVES**: 4

DIRECTIONS:

1. Warm up your air fryer to 180 degrees Celsius.
2. Mix cabbage, carrots, bell pepper, coriander, plus spring onions in your big container.
3. Put mixed vegetables in your cooking basket. Cook within ten mins, mixing once. Remove, cool it down, then move it to your big container.
4. Meanwhile, mix peanut butter, soy sauce, vinegar, honey, sesame oil, plus juice till smooth.
5. Mix cooked vegetables plus dressing till blended. Serve.

INGREDIENTS:

300 grams shredded mixed cabbage
100 grams julienned carrots
50 grams thinly sliced red bell pepper
20 grams chopped each coriander leaves & spring onions

Peanut dressing:
150 millilitres smooth peanut butter
50 millilitres each soy sauce & rice vinegar
30 millilitres honey
5 millilitres toasted sesame oil
30 millilitres lime juice

NUTRITIONAL VALUES (PER SERVING): CALORIES: 358, CARBS: 27G, FAT: 24G, PROTEIN: 12G

INGREDIENTS:

200 grams quinoa
500 millilitres water
100 grams each halved cherry tomatoes & diced cucumber
50 grams parsley, chopped
25 grams mint, chopped
50 millilitres each lemon juice & olive oil
Salt & pepper, as required

Tabbouleh with Quinoa
& FRESH HERBS
(MEDITERRANEAN)

🕐 **PREP**: 15 min   📟 **COOK**: 25 min   🍴 **SERVES**: 4

DIRECTIONS:

1. Boil your saucepan with water plus quinoa. Adjust to a simmer, then cook within fifteen mins. Fluff quinoa, then cool it down.
2. Mix tomatoes, cucumber, parsley, plus mint in your big container. Add cooled quinoa, then mix again.
3. Mix juice plus oil in your small container. Flavour it using salt plus pepper. Add it on tabbouleh mixture, then mix well.
4. Grease your cooking basket using oil. Warm up your air fryer to 180 degrees Celsius.
5. Put tabbouleh into your cooking basket, then cook within ten mins, mixing often. Serve.

NUTRITIONAL VALUES (PER SERVING): CALORIES: 340, CARBS: 40G, FAT: 15G, PROTEIN: 9G

Provencal Niçoise
SALAD (MEDITERRANEAN)

🕐 **PREP**: 15 min   📷 **COOK**: 15 min   🍴 **SERVES**: 4

DIRECTIONS:

1. Cook baby potatoes in your cooking basket at 180 degrees Celsius within ten mins.
2. Boil your small saucepan with water, then cook eggs within seven mins. Remove, then cool it down. Peel, then slice into half.
3. Blanch green beans in boiling water within two mins. Strain, wash, then put aside.
4. Mix oil, juice, garlic, salt plus pepper in your small container.
5. Mix tomatoes plus onion in your big salad container. Add potatoes, green beans plus olives. Top using flaked tuna, plus eggs.
6. Add dressing, then slowly mix. Serve.

INGREDIENTS:

400 grams baby potatoes, halved
Four medium eggs
200 grams each trimmed green beans
& halved cherry tomatoes
50 grams onion, sliced
20 black olives
200 grams tuna in spring water,
strained & flaked

For the dressing:
60 millilitres olive oil
30 millilitres lemon juice
Three grams clove garlic, minced
Salt & pepper, as required

NUTRITIONAL VALUES (PER SERVING): CALORIES: 445, CARBS: 35G, FAT: 26G, PROTEIN: 27G.

Rice Noodle
SALAD (ORIENTAL)

🕐 **PREP**: 20 min   📷 **COOK**: 10 min   🍴 **SERVES**: 4

DIRECTIONS:

1. Warm up your air fryer to 200 degrees Celsius.
2. Flavour chicken thighs using salt plus pepper.
3. Put seasoned chicken thighs in your cooking basket, then cook within ten mins, flipping once. Remove, cool it down, then slice into strips.
4. Meanwhile, boil two litres water in your big pot. Add rice noodles, then cook till tender. Strain, then wash.
5. In your small container, mix lime juice, fish & soy sauce, plus honey.
6. Lay out rice noodles in your big container. Top it using sliced chicken, carrots, cucumber, bean sprouts, mint, plus cilantro. Add dressing, then toss slowly. Serve.

INGREDIENTS:

200 grams rice noodles
500 grams no bones & skin chicken thighs
Two litres water
100 grams bean sprouts, grated carrots & sliced thinly
cucumber
50 grams each chopped cilantro & mint leaves
50 millilitres each lime juice & fish sauce
20 millilitres soy sauce
30 millilitres honey
Salt & pepper, as required

NUTRITIONAL VALUES (PER SERVING): CALORIES: 460, CARBS: 56G, FAT: 10G, PROTEIN: 35G

Ecuadorian Quinoa & AVOCADO SALAD (SOUTH AMERICAN)

🕐 **PREP**: 20 min   📷 **COOK**: 30 min   🍴 **SERVES**: 4

DIRECTIONS:

1. Boil water in your medium saucepan, add quinoa, then cook fifteen mins till tender. Strain, then put aside.
2. Warm up your air fryer to 180 degrees Celsius.
3. Put cooked quinoa into your cooking basket, then cook within fifteen mins, shaking once.
4. Meanwhile, mix quinoa, avocado, tomatoes, onion, corn, plus cilantro in your big container.
5. In your separate small container, mix juice, oil, salt, plus pepper. Add it on salad, then toss again. Serve.

INGREDIENTS:

200 grams quinoa, washed
One litre water
One cubed avocado
150 grams cherry tomatoes, halved
100 grams red onion, finely chopped
100 grams cooked corn kernels
50 grams cilantro, chopped
One lime juiced
30 millilitres olive oil
Salt & pepper, as required

NUTRITIONAL VALUES (PER SERVING): CALORIES: 550, CARBS: 63G, FAT: 24G, PROTEIN: 12G

Brazilian Brigadeiro (SOUTH AMERICAN)

🕐 **PREP**: 15 min   📷 **COOK**: 10 min   🍴 **SERVES**: 20

DIRECTIONS:

1. Mix condensed milk, cocoa, plus butter on low temp in your medium saucepan till it thickens.
2. Remove, then mix in vanilla extract. Cool it down in your fridge. Shape cooled mixture into small balls, roll each into chocolate sprinkles.
3. Warm up your air fryer to 180 degrees Celsius.
4. Put brigadeiro balls in your oiled cooking basket. Cook within five mins till warmed, shaking once. Remove, cool it down, then serve.

INGREDIENTS:

200 grams condensed milk, sweetened
50 grams cocoa powder, unsweetened
30 grams butter, unsalted
Five millilitres vanilla extract
200 grams chocolate sprinkles
Fifteen millilitres vegetable oil

NUTRITIONAL VALUES (PER SERVING): CALORIES 187, CARBS 22G, FAT 10G, PROTEIN 3G

Chinese Almond
COOKIES (ORIENTAL)

🕐 **PREP**: 20 min   ▥ **COOK**: 10 min   🍴 **SERVES**: 4

DIRECTIONS:

1. Mix butter plus sugar in your big container till creamy. Mix in egg yolk plus almond extract.
2. Mix flour, almonds, plus salt in your separate container. Combine it butter mixture till a soft dough forms. Split it into sixteen, then roll each into a ball.
3. Flatten them slightly, put on your lined plate, then press almond into each centre.
4. Warm up your air fryer to 180 degrees Celsius. Put cookies in your cooking basket, then cook within ten mins till lightly golden. Remove, cool it down, then serve.

INGREDIENTS:

200 grams flour, all-purpose
100 grams butter, unsalted, softened
75 grams sugar, granulated
One egg yolk
40 grams almonds, ground
25 grams almonds, whole
Five millilitres almond extract
Salt, as required

NUTRITIONAL VALUES (PER SERVING): CALORIES 425, CARBS 48G, FAT 21G, PROTEIN 8G

INGREDIENTS:

200 grams mascarpone cheese
100 grams sugar, granulated
Two big eggs, separated
250 millilitres espresso, cooled
200 grams ladyfinger biscuits
Two grams cocoa powder, unsweetened
150 grams heavy cream

Tiramisu with Mascarpone
& ESPRESSO (MEDITERRANEAN)

🕐 **PREP**: 15 min   ▥ **COOK**: 10 min   🍴 **SERVES**: 4

DIRECTIONS:

1. Mix mascarpone plus half of sugar in your medium container till smooth.
2. Beat egg yolks plus rest of sugar using your electric mixer till creamy. Fold it into your mascarpone mixture, mixing well.
3. In your separate container, beat egg whites till stiff, then fold them into your mascarpone mixture.
4. Add cooled espresso in your shallow container. Dip each ladyfinger biscuit slightly into your espresso mixture, then layer in your baking dish.
5. Put half of mascarpone mixture on ladyfingers. Put another soaked ladyfinger layer, then add rest of mascarpone mixture on top.
6. Whip heavy cream to soft peaks, then spread it on top. Dust it using cocoa powder. Serve.

NUTRITIONAL VALUES (PER SERVING): CALORIES 830, CARBS 87G, FAT 46G, PROTEIN 16G

Greek Baklava with
HONEY & WALNUTS (MEDITERRANEAN)

🕐 **PREP:** 30 min   ▣ **COOK:** 20 min   🍴 **SERVES:** 12

DIRECTIONS:

1. Warm up your air fryer to 160 degrees Celsius.
2. Mix walnuts plus one-third sugar in your container, then put aside.
3. Brush your baking pan using butter. Put two phyllo sheets in it, then brush using butter. Do same using seven phyllo sheets plus butter.
4. Spread walnut mixture on top. Layer again using rest phyllo sheets plus butter, then slice it into diamond shapes.
5. Put baking pan into your cooking basket, then cook within twenty mins till golden.
6. Meanwhile, mix water, honey, rest of sugar, zest plus juice in your saucepan on moderate temp, mixing often. Remove, then cool it down.
7. Pour it on hot baklava, cool it down, then serve.

INGREDIENTS:

300 grams phyllo pastry sheets
300 grams walnuts, chopped
200 grams unsalted butter, dissolved
160 grams sugar
125 millilitres water
250 millilitres honey
One litre each orange zest & lemon juice

NUTRITIONAL VALUES (PER SERVING): CALORIES 486, CARBS 48G, FAT 30G, PROTEIN 7G

Japanese Matcha
MOCHI (ORIENTAL)

🕐 **PREP:** 15 min   ▣ **COOK:** 10 min   🍴 **SERVES:** 4

INGREDIENTS:

200 grams rice flour, glutinous
60 grams sugar, granulated
240 millilitres water
Two grams green tea powder, matcha
100 grams red bean paste

DIRECTIONS:

1. Whisk flour, sugar, plus green tea powder in your medium container. Slowly pour water while mixing till smooth. Fold in red bean paste. Form it into small balls.
2. Warm up your air fryer to 180 degrees Celsius.
3. Put mochi balls into your oiled cooking basket, then cook within ten mins till slightly crispy. Remove, cool it down, then serve.

NUTRITIONAL VALUES (PER SERVING): CALORIES 380, CARBS 80G, FAT 2G, PROTEIN 5G

CONCLUSION

You can see by now that it takes the easy and convenient way of preparing foods of all sorts with many varied palates.

Finally, our last piece of advice is that you ought to keep on trying out new things the many things that air fryers can do. This book provides the base recipe for air fried snacks; however, you may take your skills a notch higher, explore more avenues and add in these recipes while maintaining the healthiness of the traditional meals.

Also, don't forget that you can pass your knowledge to your relatives and friends. Let them know about a new approach, using an air-fryer in their cooking process at homes. Eating together with loved ones makes every pleasure of cooking and every tasty morsel doubly enjoyable.

You can also re-work recipes based on personalized preferences in terms of ingredients, spices, and cooking time. Doing so will open a way for one to invent personalized dishes to meet your particular taste as well as other people that are closely related to you.

Finally, always keep in mind that "practice makes perfect". However, take your own time to assimilate its intricacies, do not get discouraged by the first errors on your way to healthy eating! Therefore, while you should have fun eating every nutritious meal, be ready to face the accompanying tasks and rejoice in the benefits attached.

We are thankful that you chose to use our book as a guide into this fantastic air-frying cooking universe. May your trip be full of sweet discoveries, long-lasting happy moments, and delicious meals that sustain and uplift your spirits. And by now grab your apron, switch on your air fryer and enjoy the flavour in every crisp, tender, and golden morsel.

HERE IS YOUR FREE GIFT!

Printed in Great Britain
by Amazon

32900710R00066